Arthur Rackham's Fairies and Nymphs:
A Vintage Grayscale Adult Coloring Book

By Ligia Ortega
ColoringPress.com

This book is dedicated to my IAWC friends. Thank you for caring, listening, offering encouragement, and for all the support you give. I am grateful for each of you.

Artist's Message

It means so much that you have chosen to purchase this book. I hope it brings you or a loved one hours of coloring pleasure.

All images in this book were lovingly sourced, curated, and restored by me. I then worked to carefully convert every image to high-quality grayscale, digitize every page and assemble them electronically to prepare for printing. This coloring book has been a true labor of love, representing months of work (plus sleep deprivation and neglect of friendships and housework!). Although the source images are public domain, the work I have done to restore and convert these images into grayscale coloring pages is protected by Copyright Law. I took the time and additional expense to officially register this book with the Copyright Office. Please respect Copyright Law.

You may:

Copy the uncolored pages on other paper preferences for yourself.
Post colored images on social media.
Give the colored pages as gifts.
Give a physical book you purchased as a gift.

You may not:

Share physical or electronic copies of uncolored pages with anyone else, whether free or for sale.
Post uncolored pages anywhere online, claim them as your own, or distribute uncolored pages via e-mail or electronic downloads.
Incorporate uncolored or colored images on items besides colored pages.
Sell uncolored or colored images, cards, or crafts made with the coloring pages, use them on products, or for any commercial usage.

ColoringGifts@yahoo.com   ColoringPress.com   www.facebook.com/ColoringPress

ISBN: 978-1530976379

ISBN: 1530976375

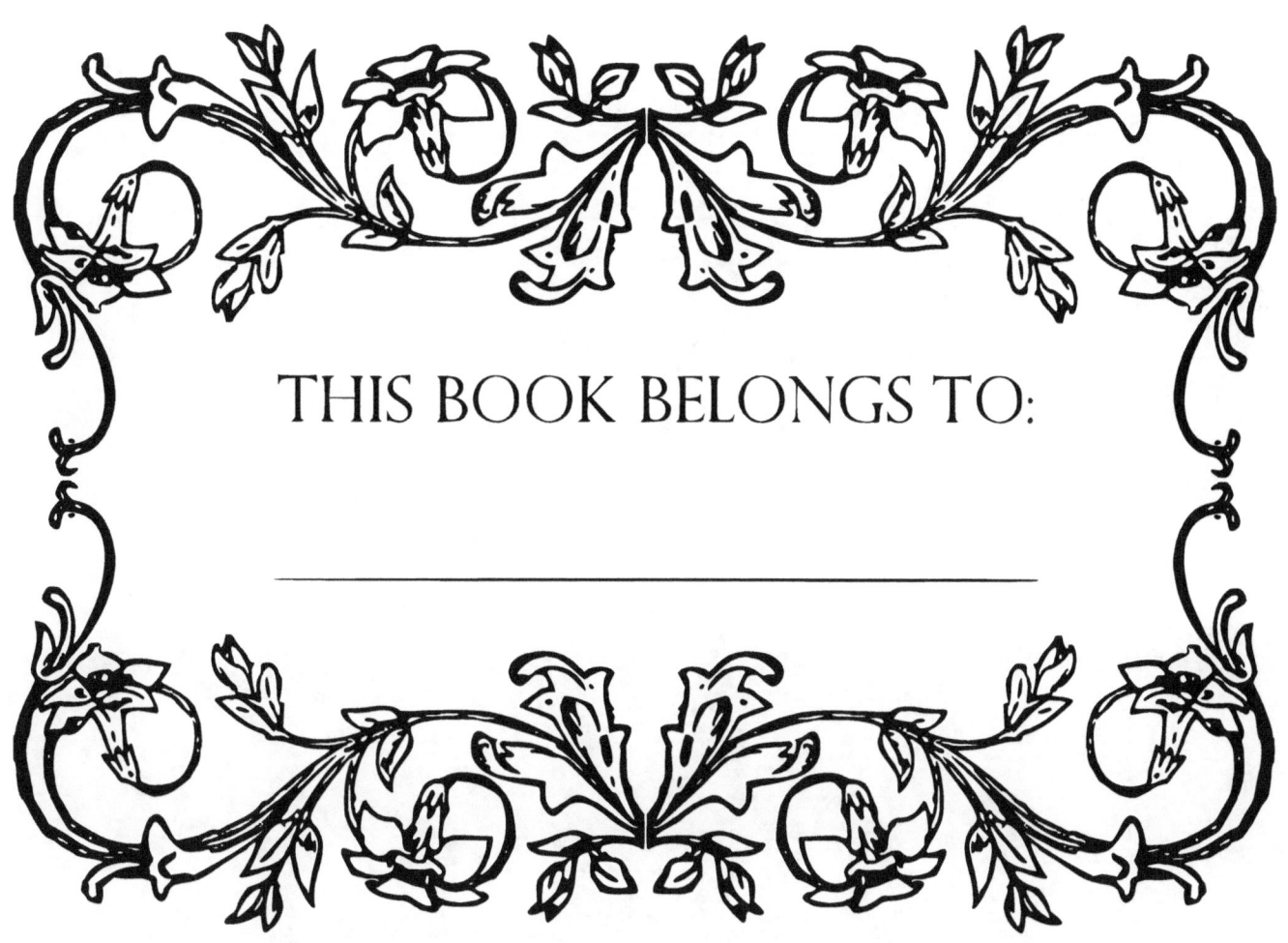

THIS BOOK BELONGS TO:

_____

ABOUT THIS BOOK

Early in my art career I was exposed to the work of several turn-of-the-century illustrators, and I discovered a few favorites whose work I spent hours poring over. One of these illustrators was Arthur Rackham. I first saw his image *Fairies have tiffs with birds* and it literally made me laugh out loud. After that, I just had to find out more about this illustrator and his work. This happened in the days before the internet, so it took some dedicated searching. The local library didn't have anything and I finally found myself digging around the stacks of the local university's fine arts library, giddy to find a book of his work. I was delighted a few years later when I finally was able to get a library card for the university's library because it meant I could actually bring some of these books home with me instead of spending hours at library stacks looking at illustrations.

While working on other adult coloring books, I remembered Arthur Rackham's work, and thought wouldn't it be wonderful to take the exquisite work done by this amazing illustrator and introduce it to a whole new generation of people? I got to work and began researching, sourcing illustrations, curating them to the best ones, and spent hours sorting them into several collections. Then the real work began. After many attempts to convert his work to line art, I decided these illustrations could not be separated from his original technique and would be best suited to the nuances of grayscale. I worked to restore the illustrations (the originals I was able to source were printed book plates, many made approximately 100 years ago, so they needed hours of work to be made into this finished book) and then finally digitizing the images to get them ready to print. I researched and learned how to make the best possible grayscale page (it's a lot more complex than simply making an image black and white) and after converting the restored, digitized illustrations to grayscale, set out to assemble the images into this book. This is the first book in a series, and I will be working on a total of six Arthur Rackham vintage grayscale adult coloring books.

Arthur Rackham (1867-1939) was one of the leading illustrators from the 'Golden Age' of British book illustrators. He had a unique style and worked in pencil, then used pens and India ink to make his drawings. If his work was to be printed in color, he added many layers of soft watercolor washes, and then to compensate for the loss of detail in printing technology at the time, he went over his drawing again with ink after painting. Like many artists of his time, he was influenced by Japanese woodblock prints and also had a visible influence from Nordic art from Northern Europe.

I am already working on the next vintage grayscale adult coloring book. Please visit my site at ColoringPress.com or find me on Facebook at facebook.com/ColoringPress to share your colored pages, to get grayscale coloring tips, and for more information on my next volumes in this series.

Thank you for choosing this volume and I hope you enjoy coloring this illustrator's delightful work!

Ligia Ortega

ILLUSTRATIONS

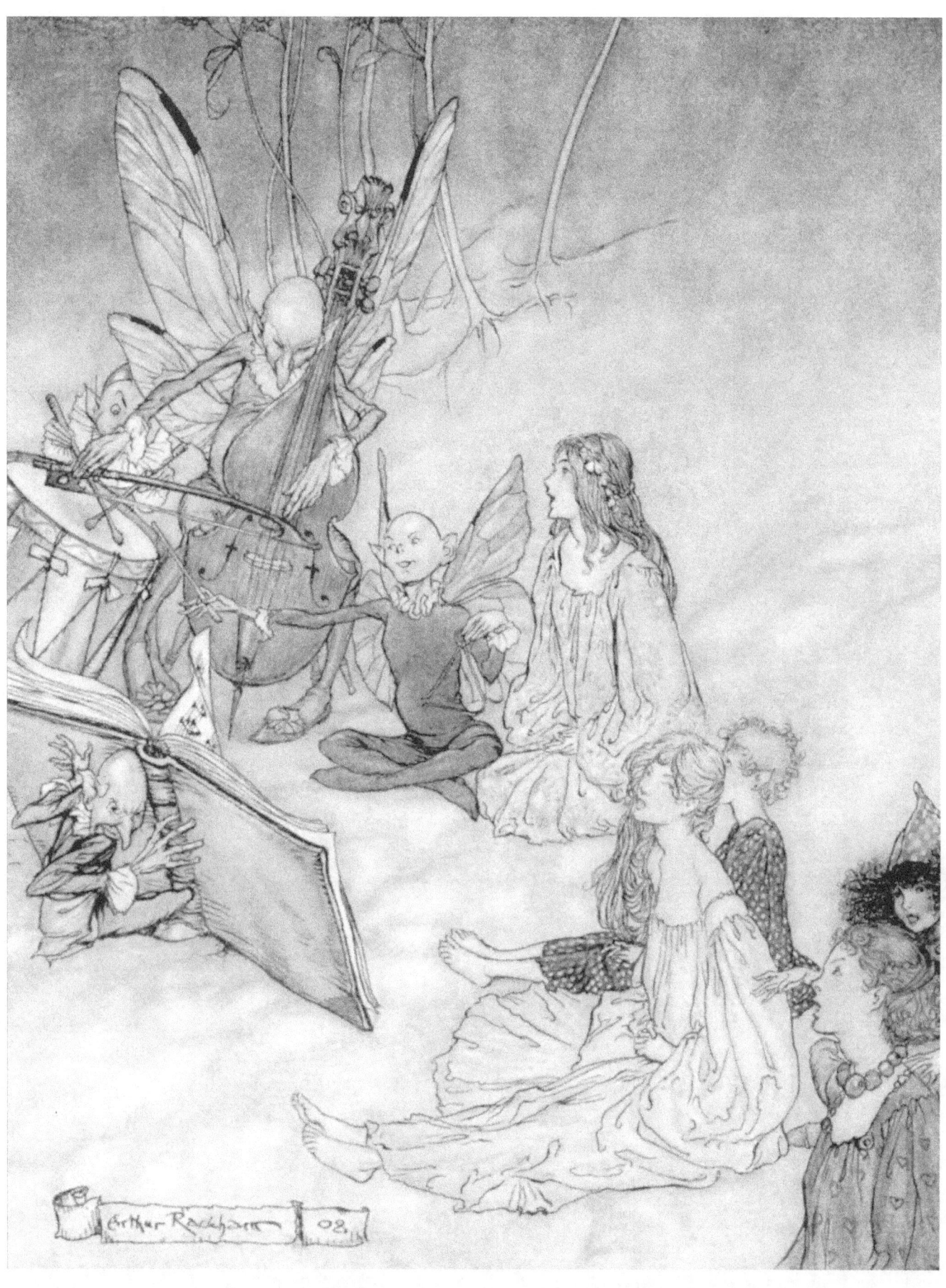

Arthur Rackham's Fairies and Nymphs

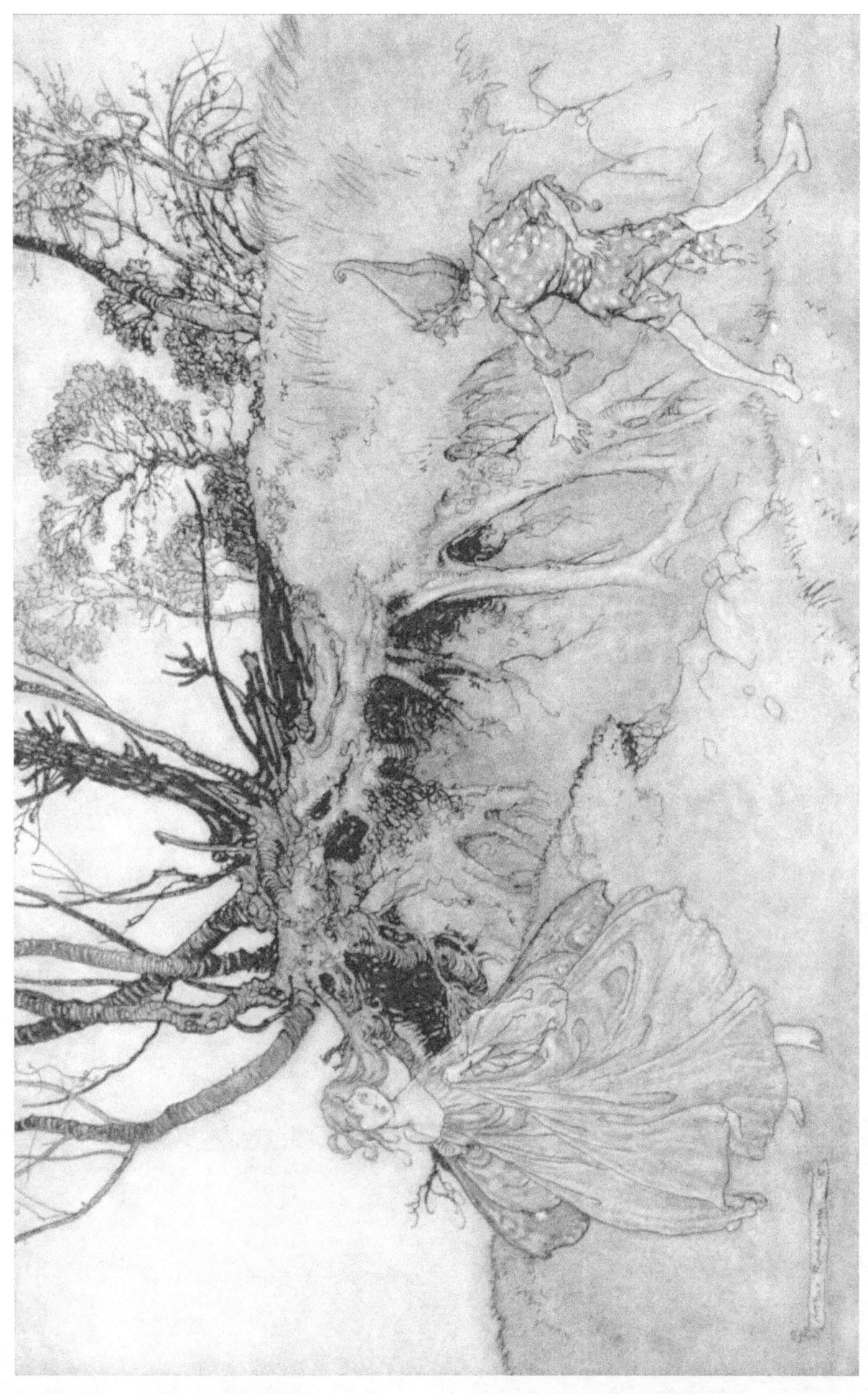

Arthur Rackham's Fairies and Nymphs   ©2016 Ligia Ortega - ColoringPress.com

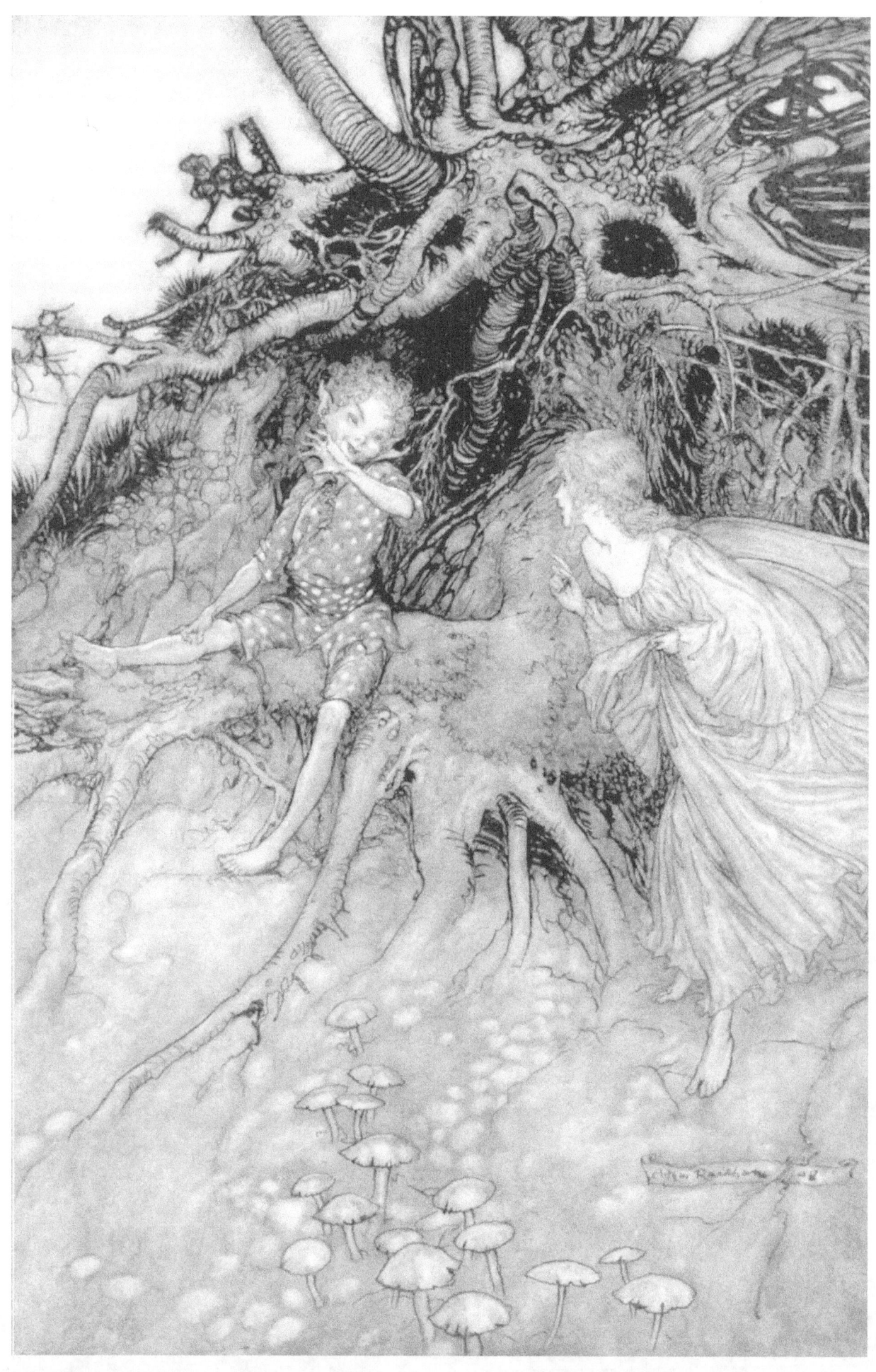

Arthur Rackham's Fairies and Nymphs

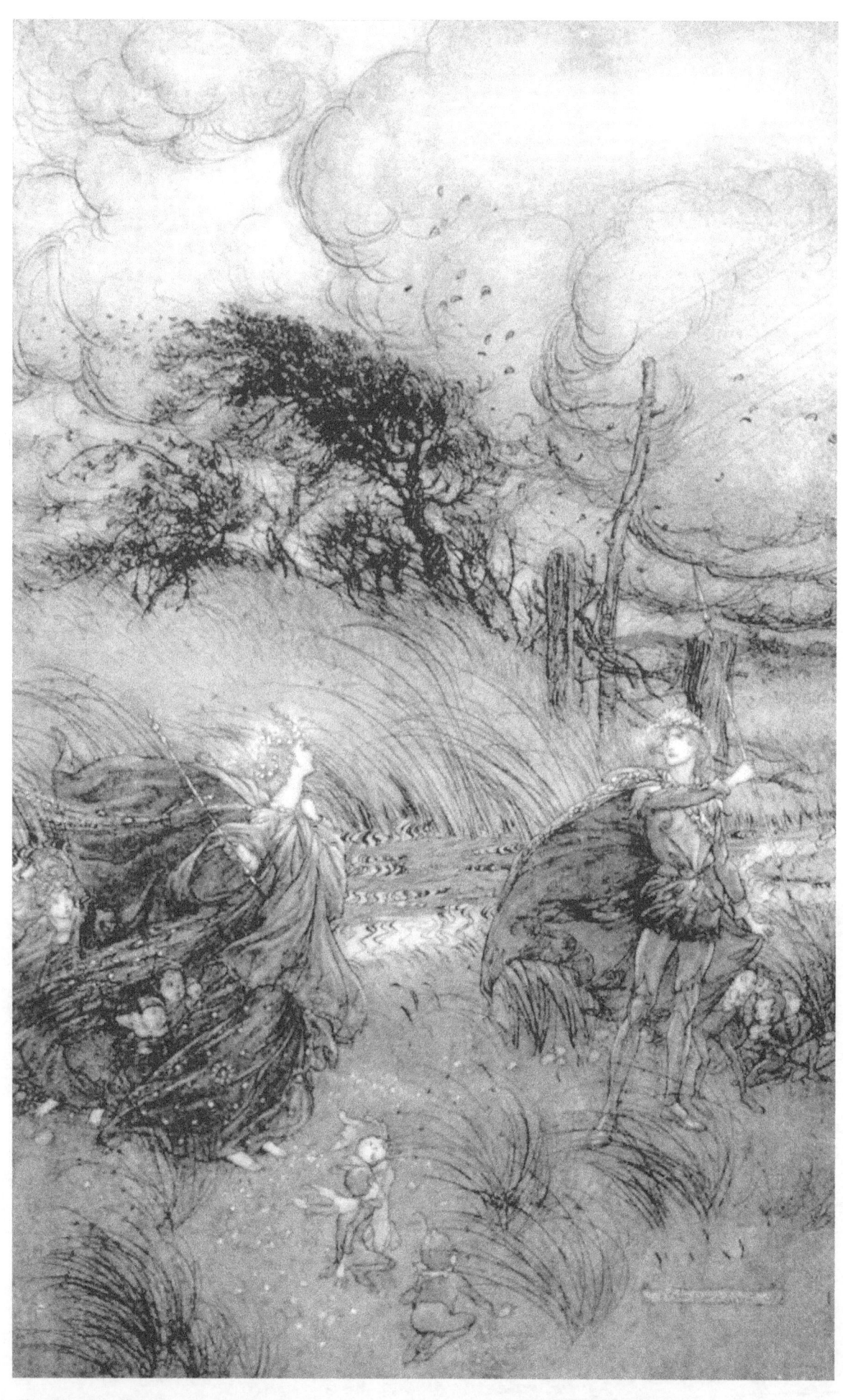

Arthur Rackham's Fairies and Nymphs

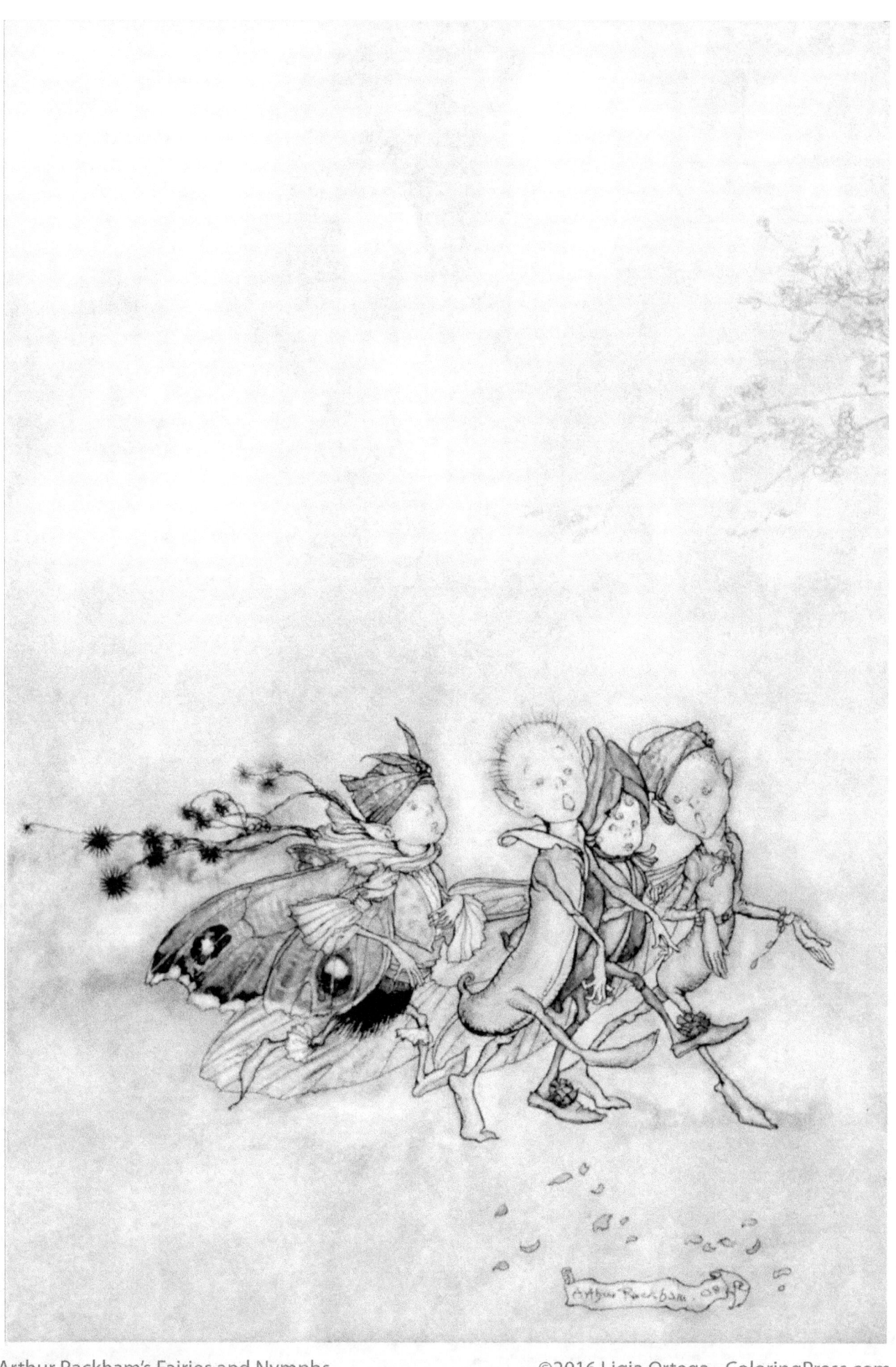

Arthur Rackham's Fairies and Nymphs

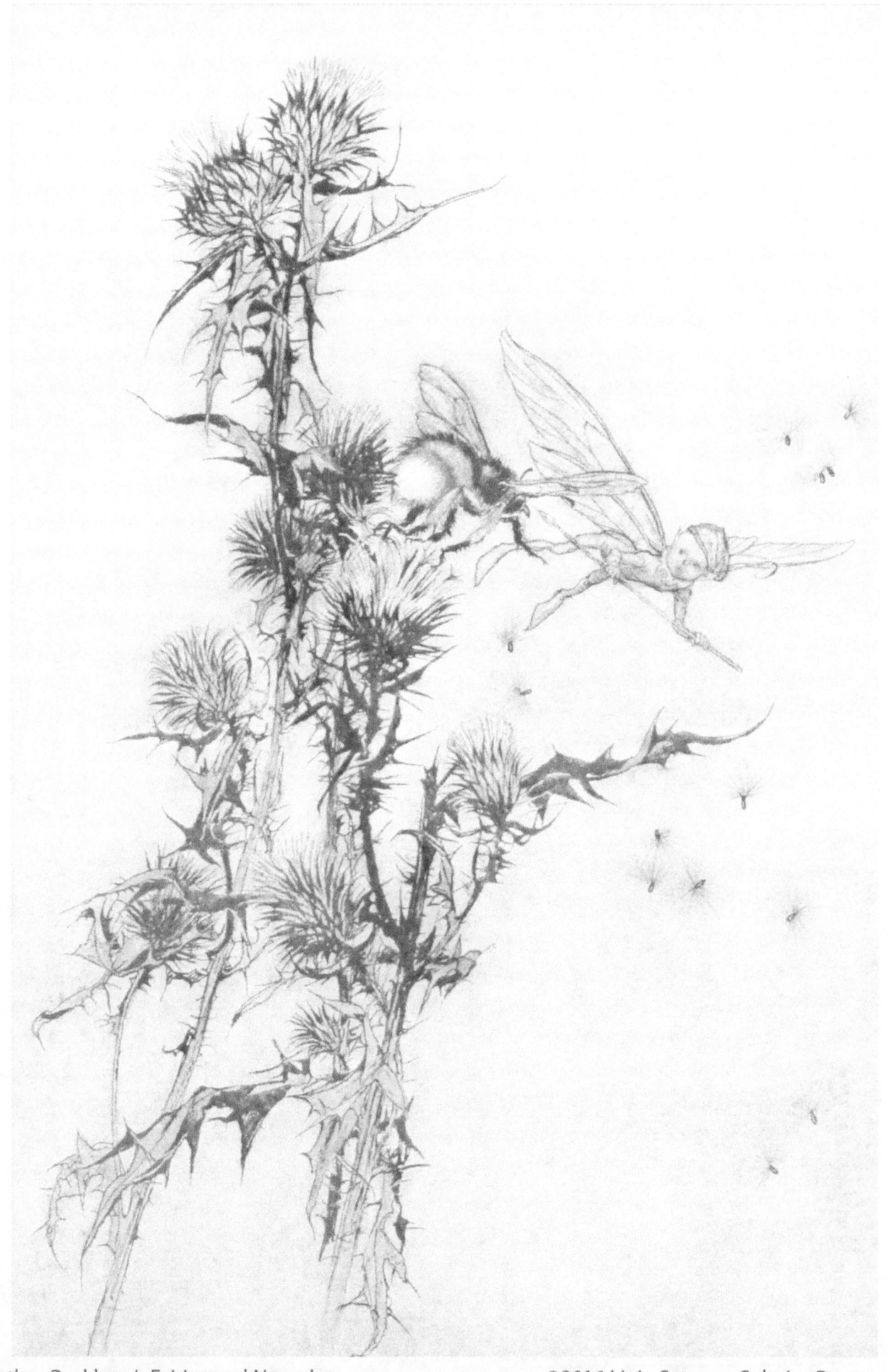

Arthur Rackham's Fairies and Nymphs

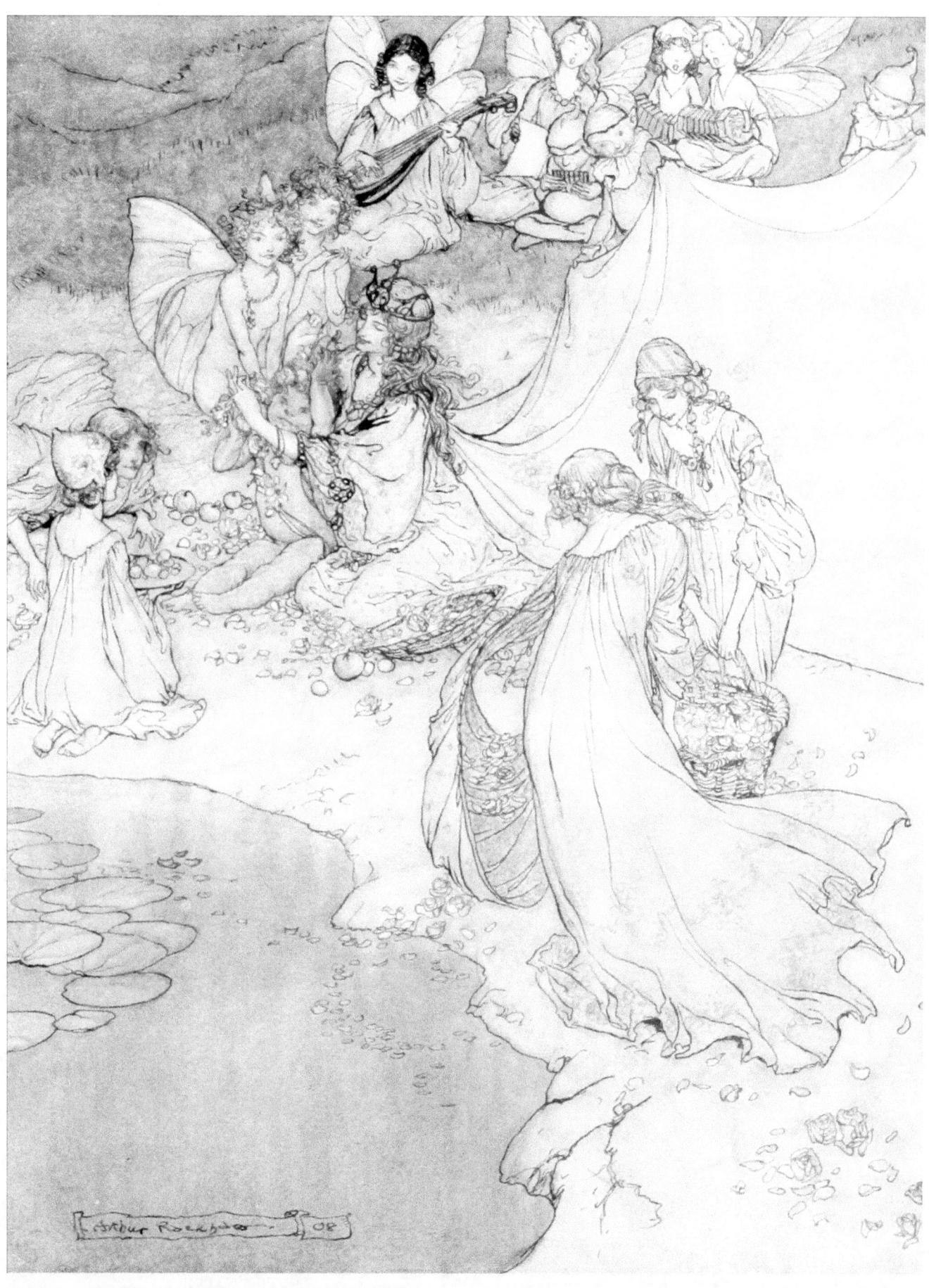

Arthur Rackham's Fairies and Nymphs

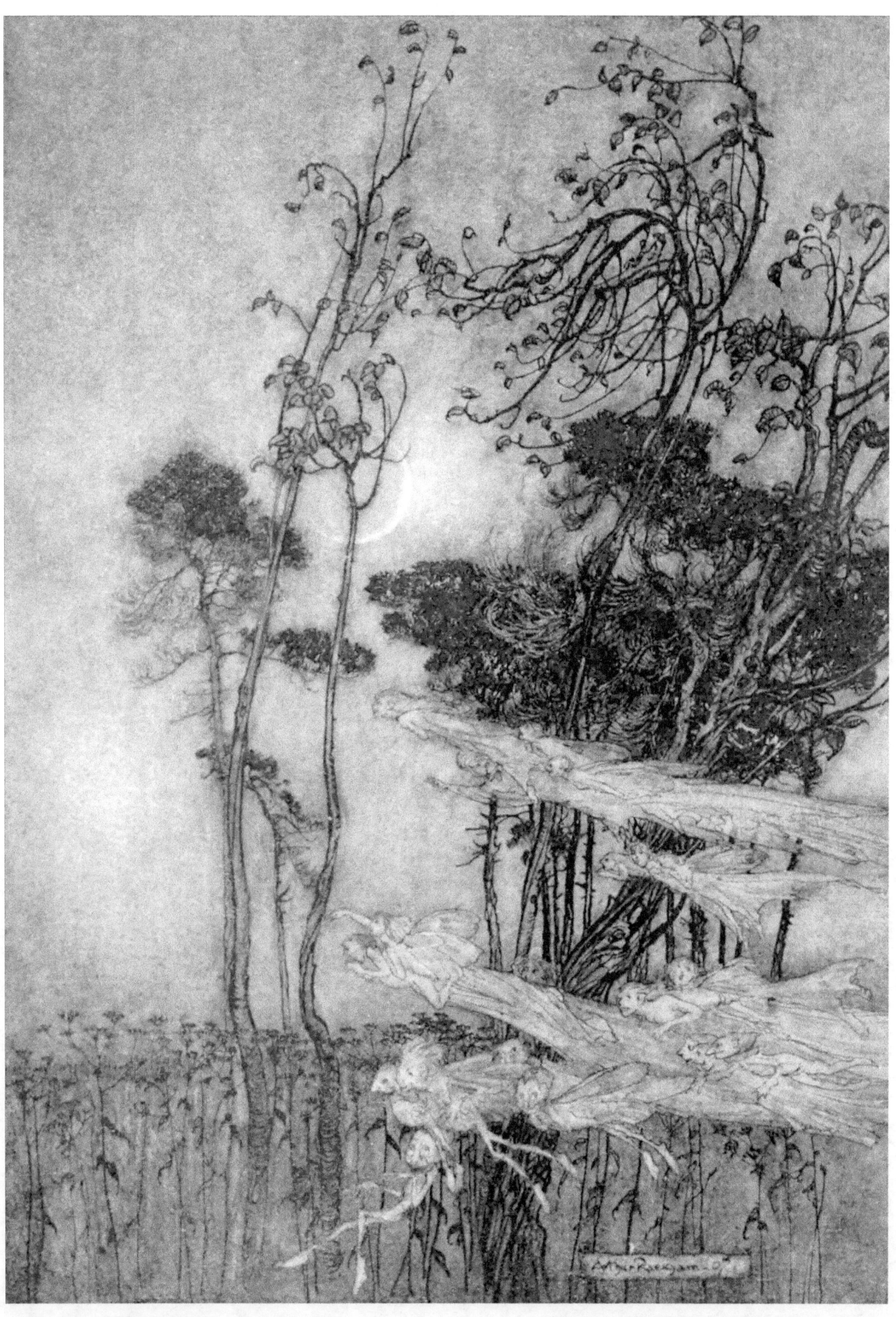

Arthur Rackham's Fairies and Nymphs

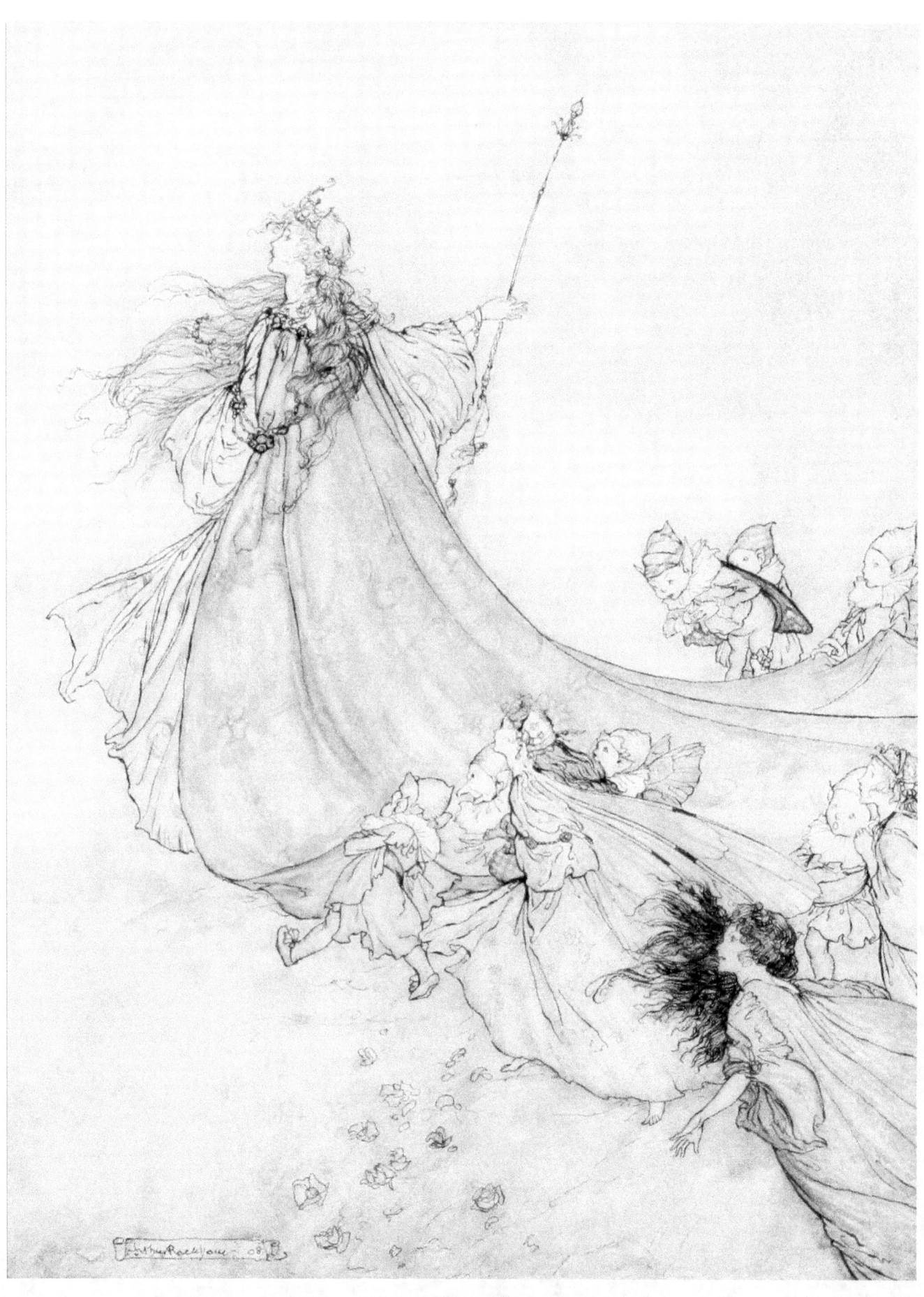

Arthur Rackham's Fairies and Nymphs

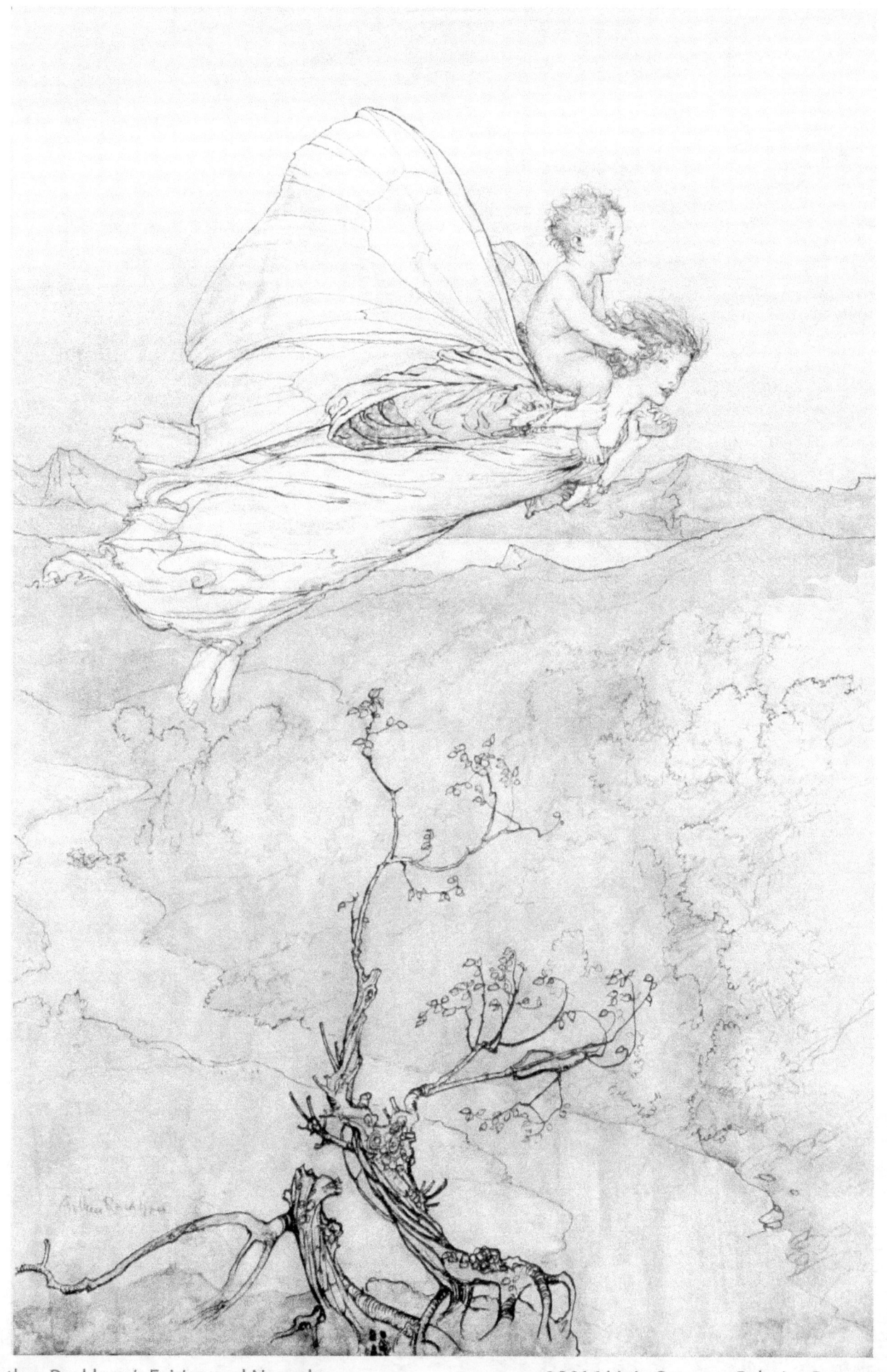

Arthur Rackham's Fairies and Nymphs   ©2016 Ligia Ortega - ColoringPress.com

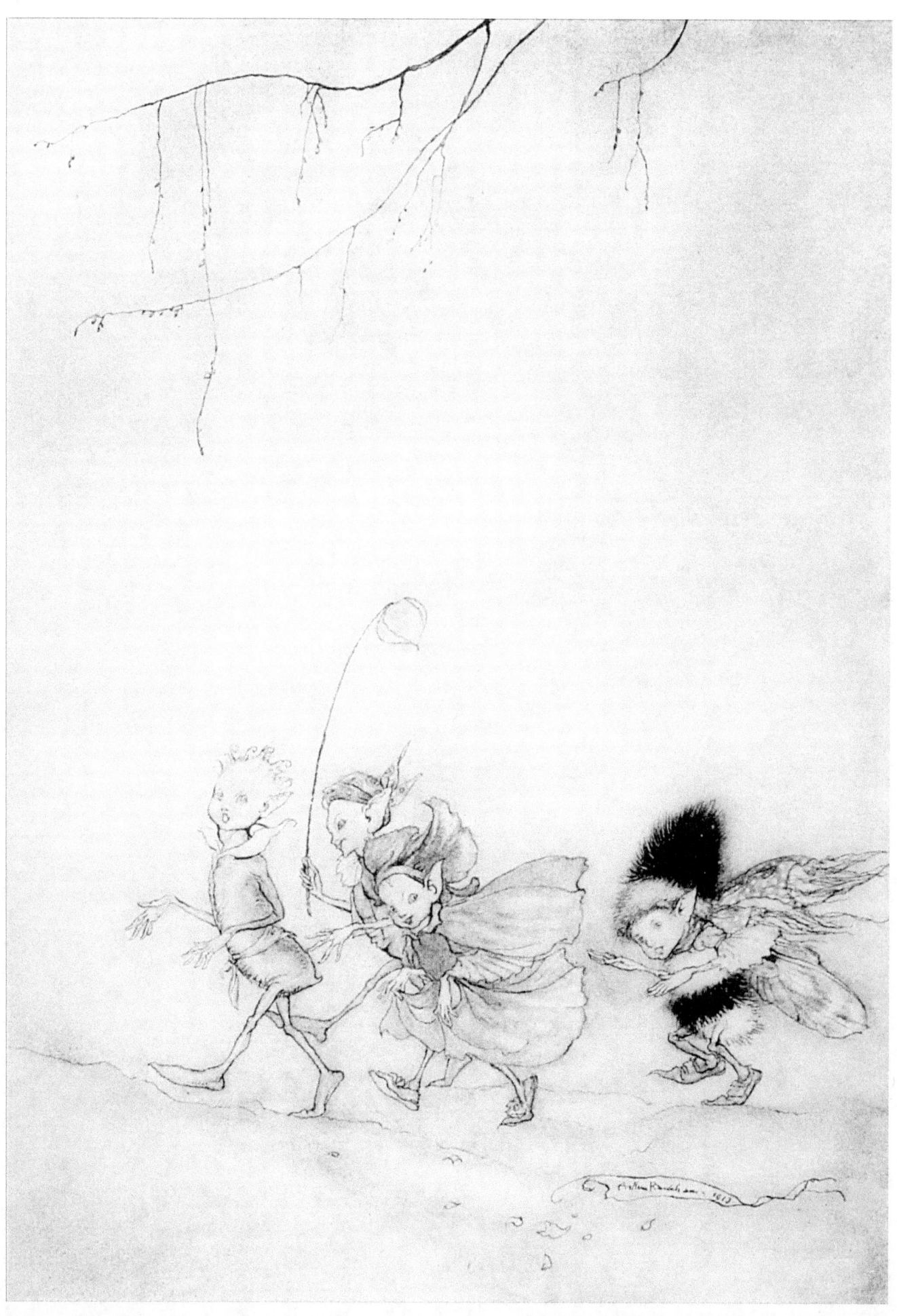

Arthur Rackham's Fairies and Nymphs   ©2016 Ligia Ortega - ColoringPress.com

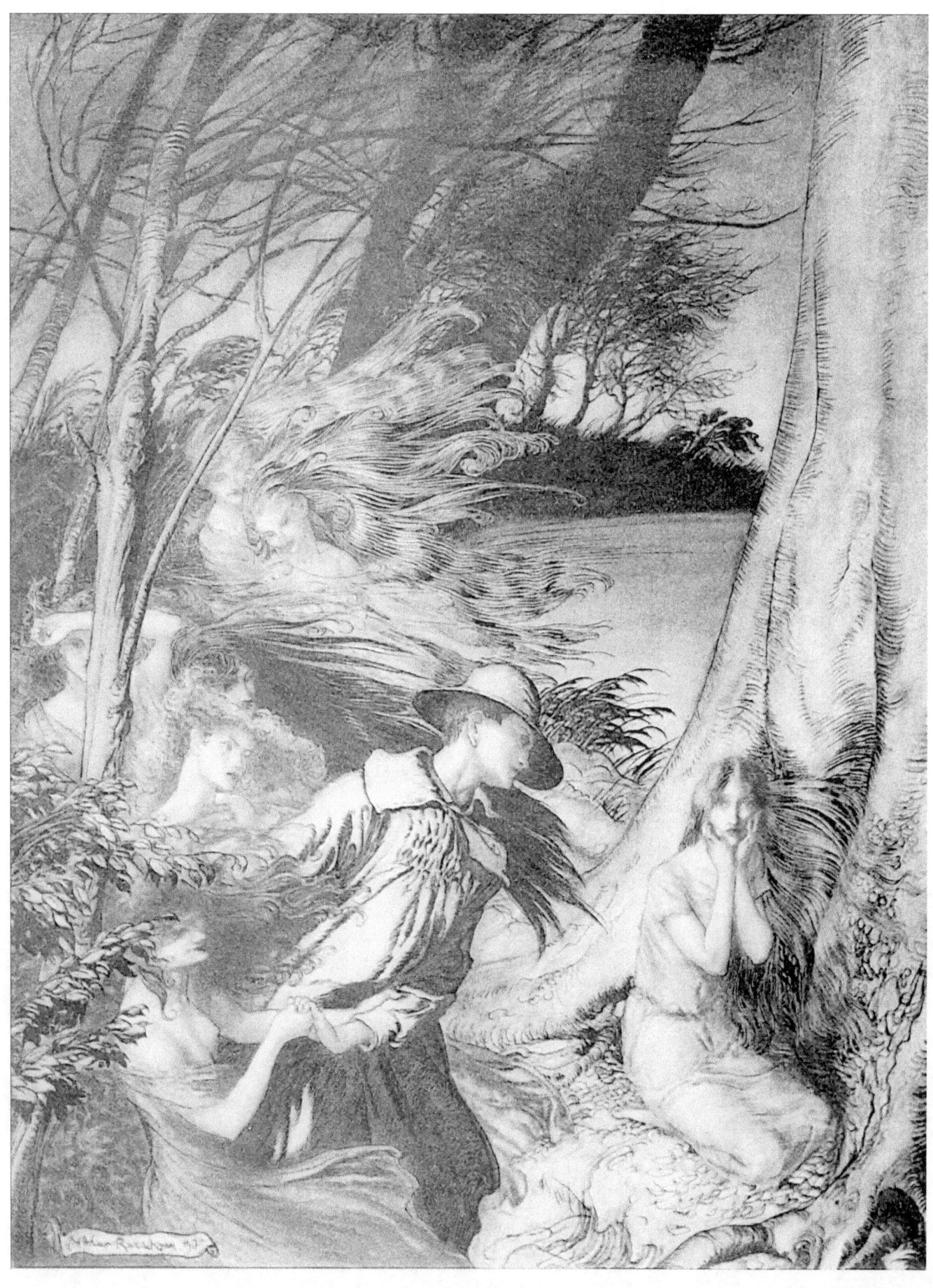

Arthur Rackham's Fairies and Nymphs

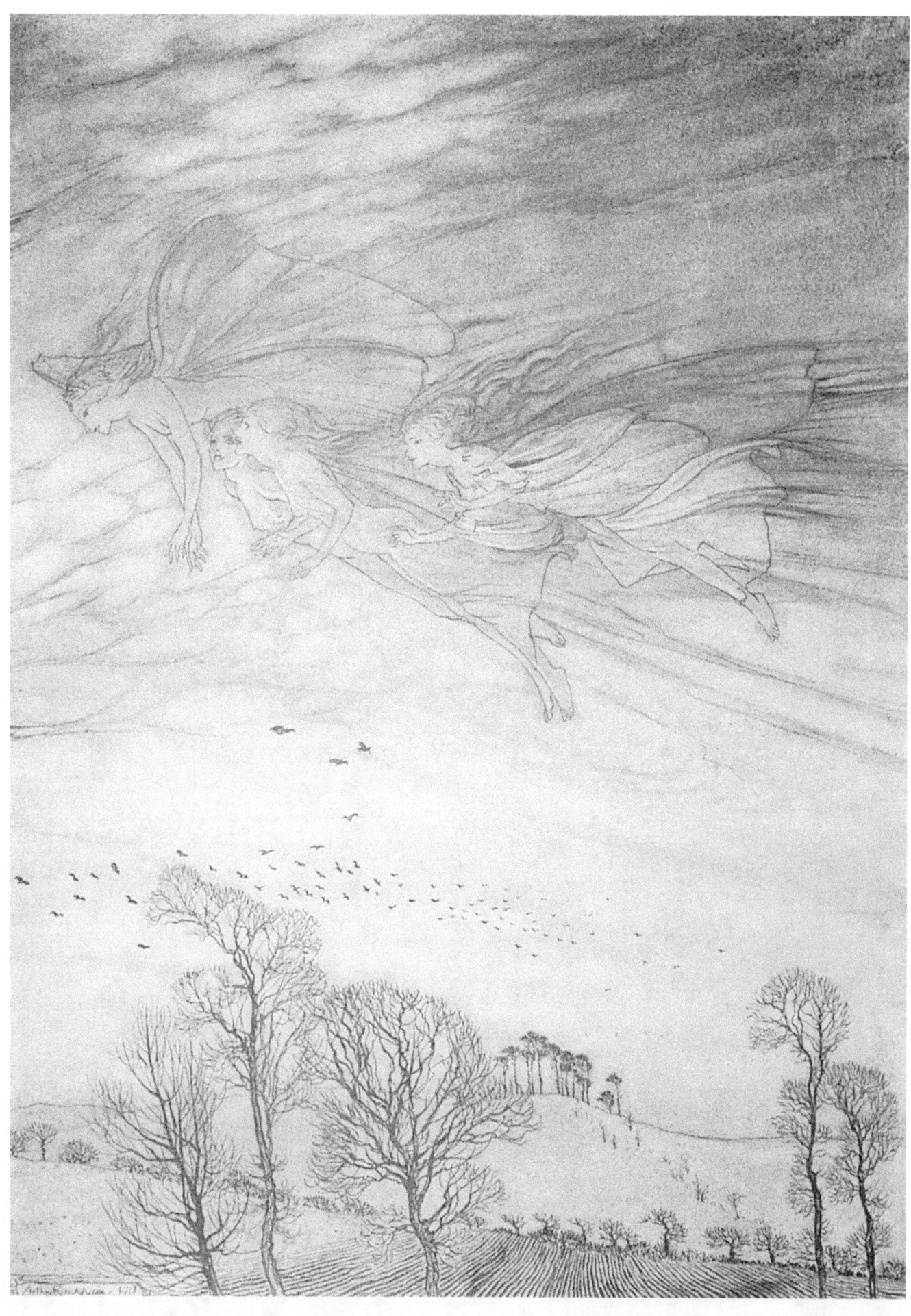

Arthur Rackham's Fairies and Nymphs

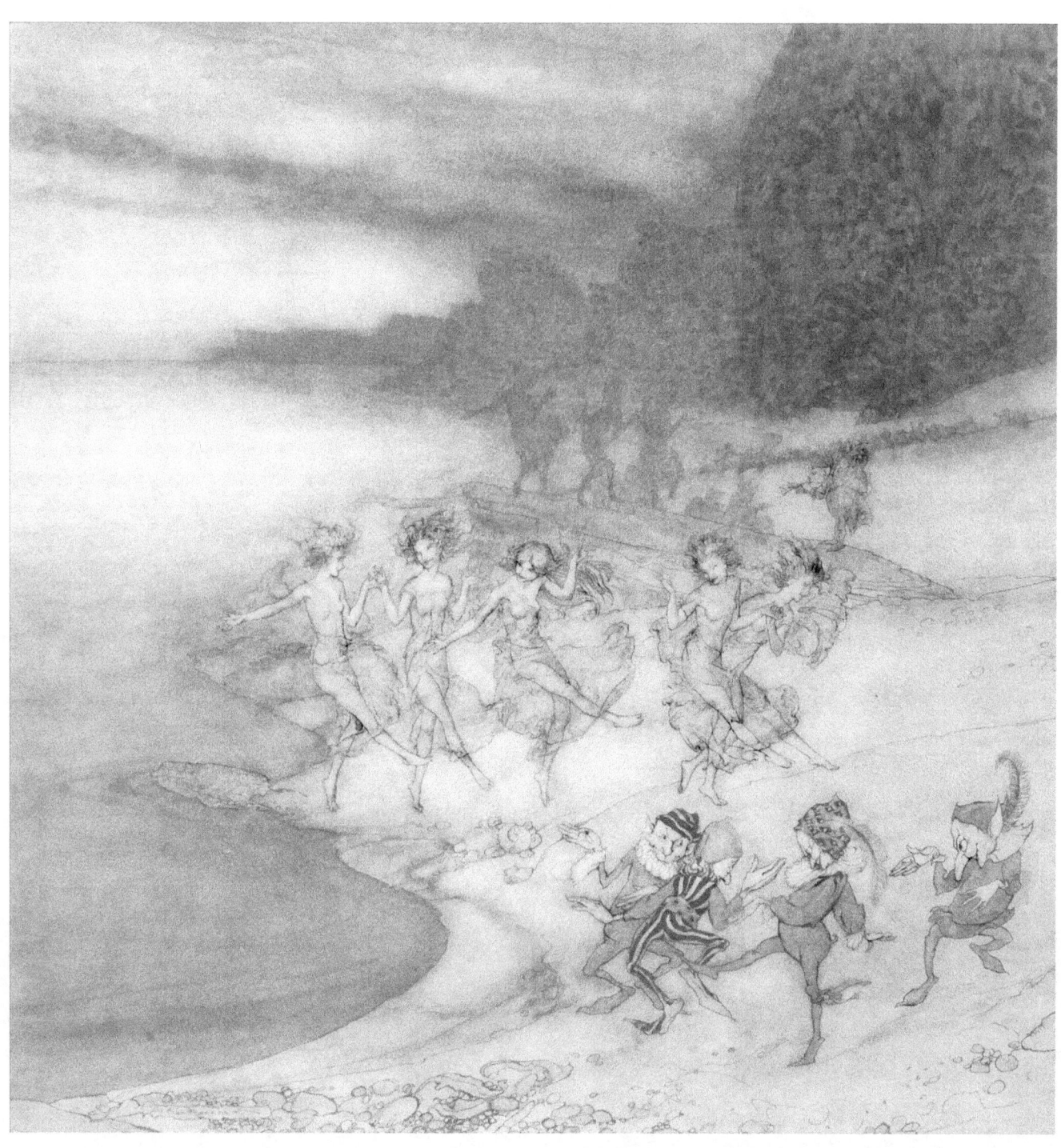

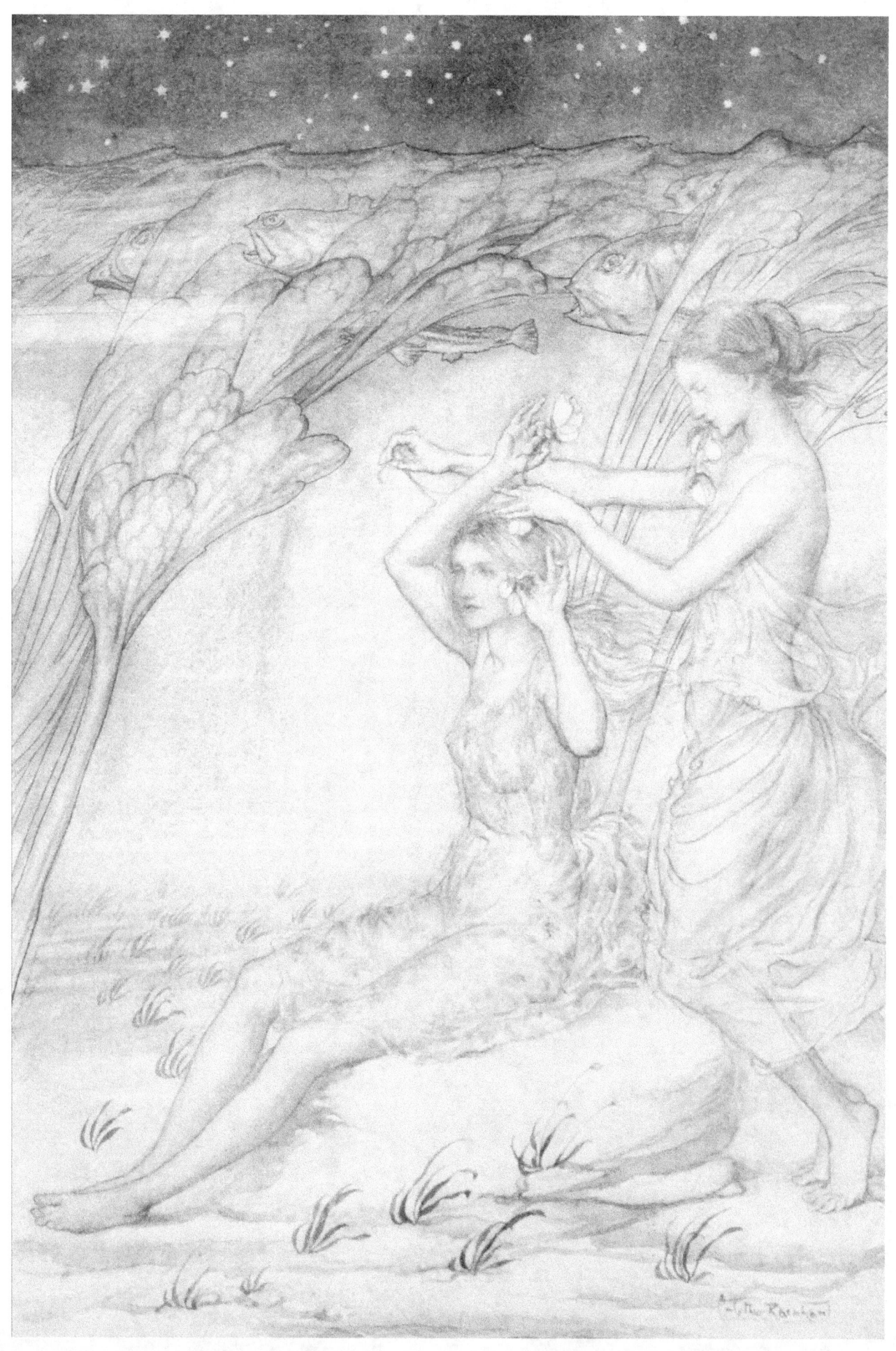

Arthur Rackham's Fairies and Nymphs   ©2016 Ligia Ortega - ColoringPress.com

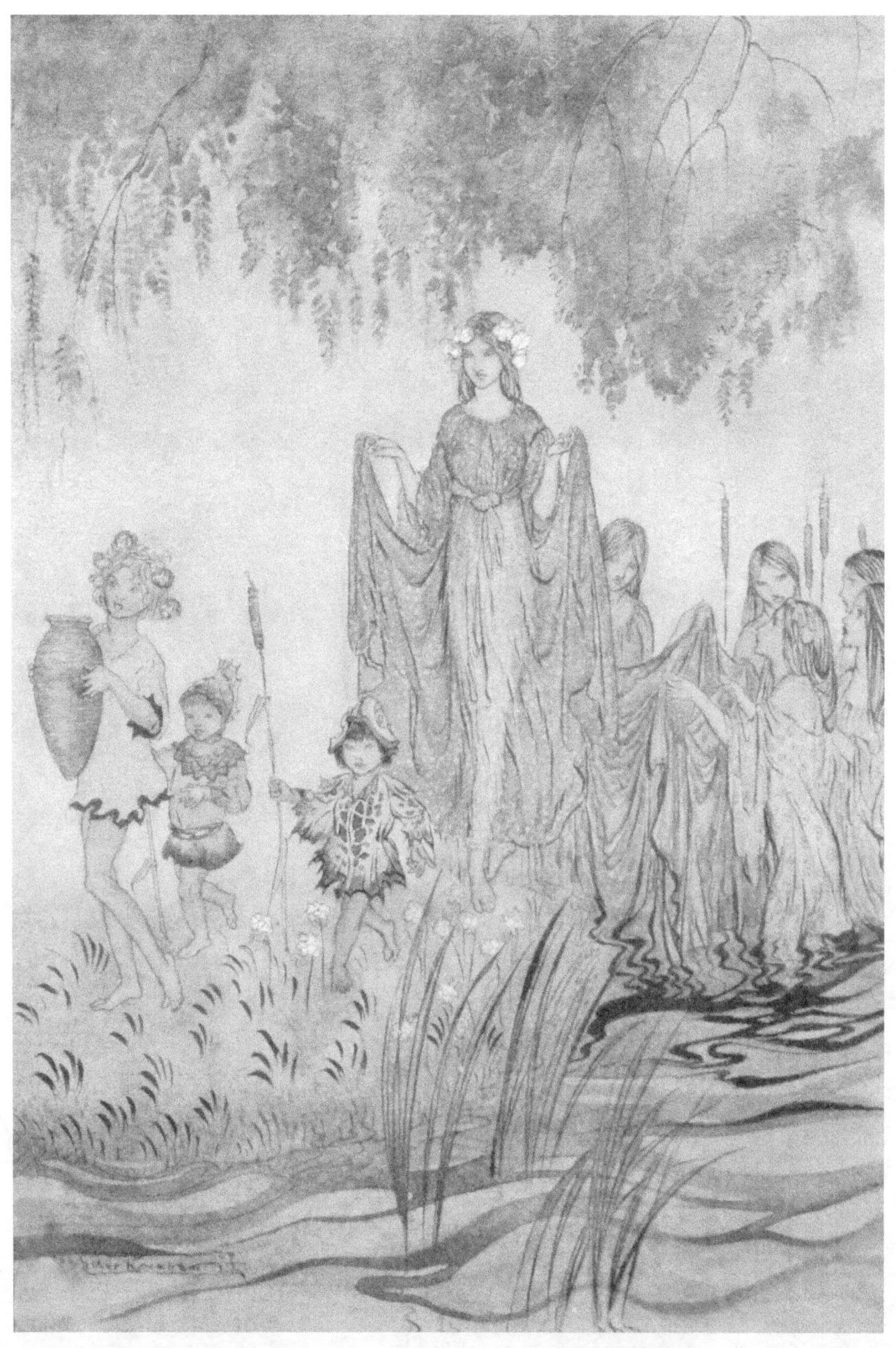

Arthur Rackham's Fairies and Nymphs

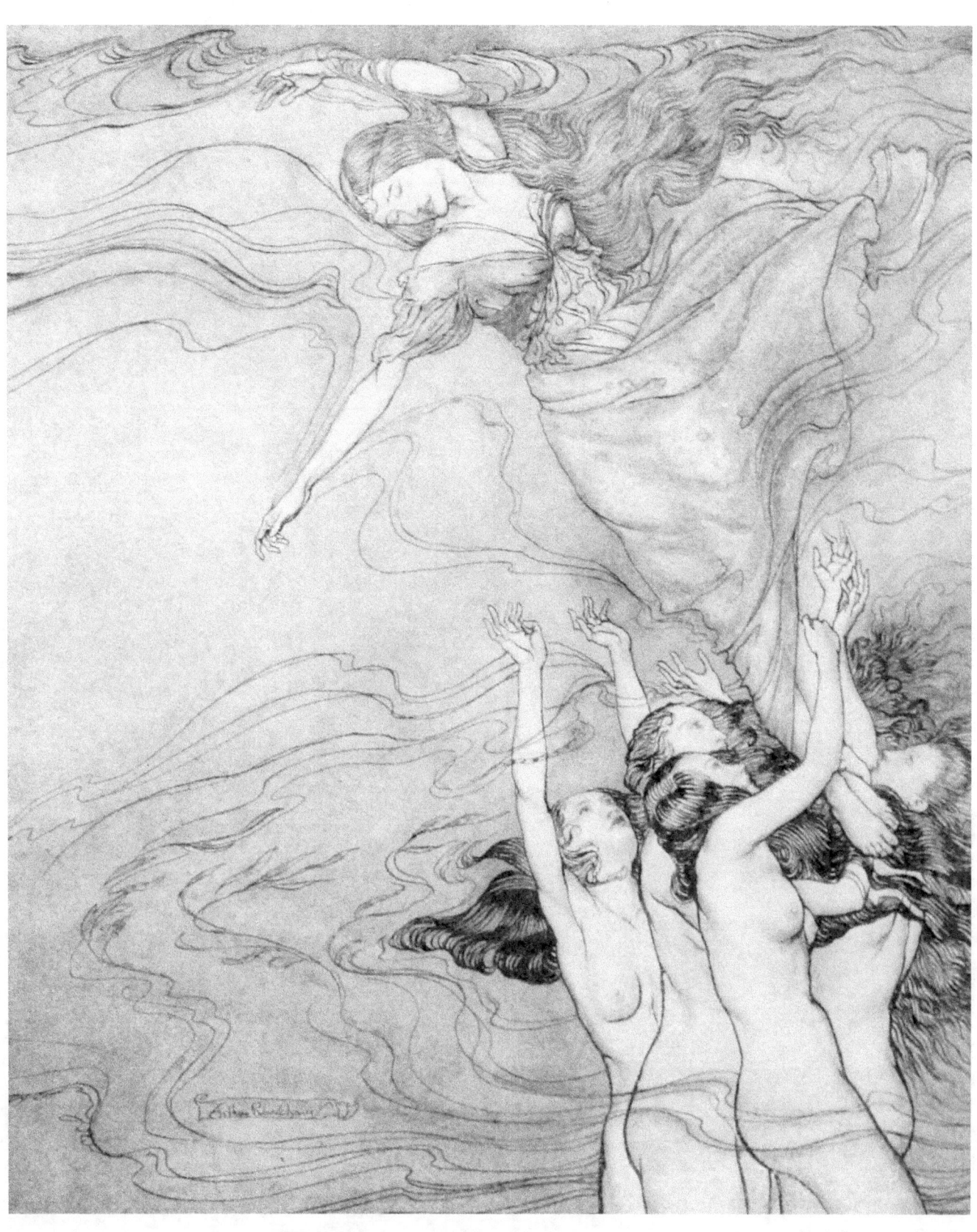

Arthur Rackham's Fairies and Nymphs

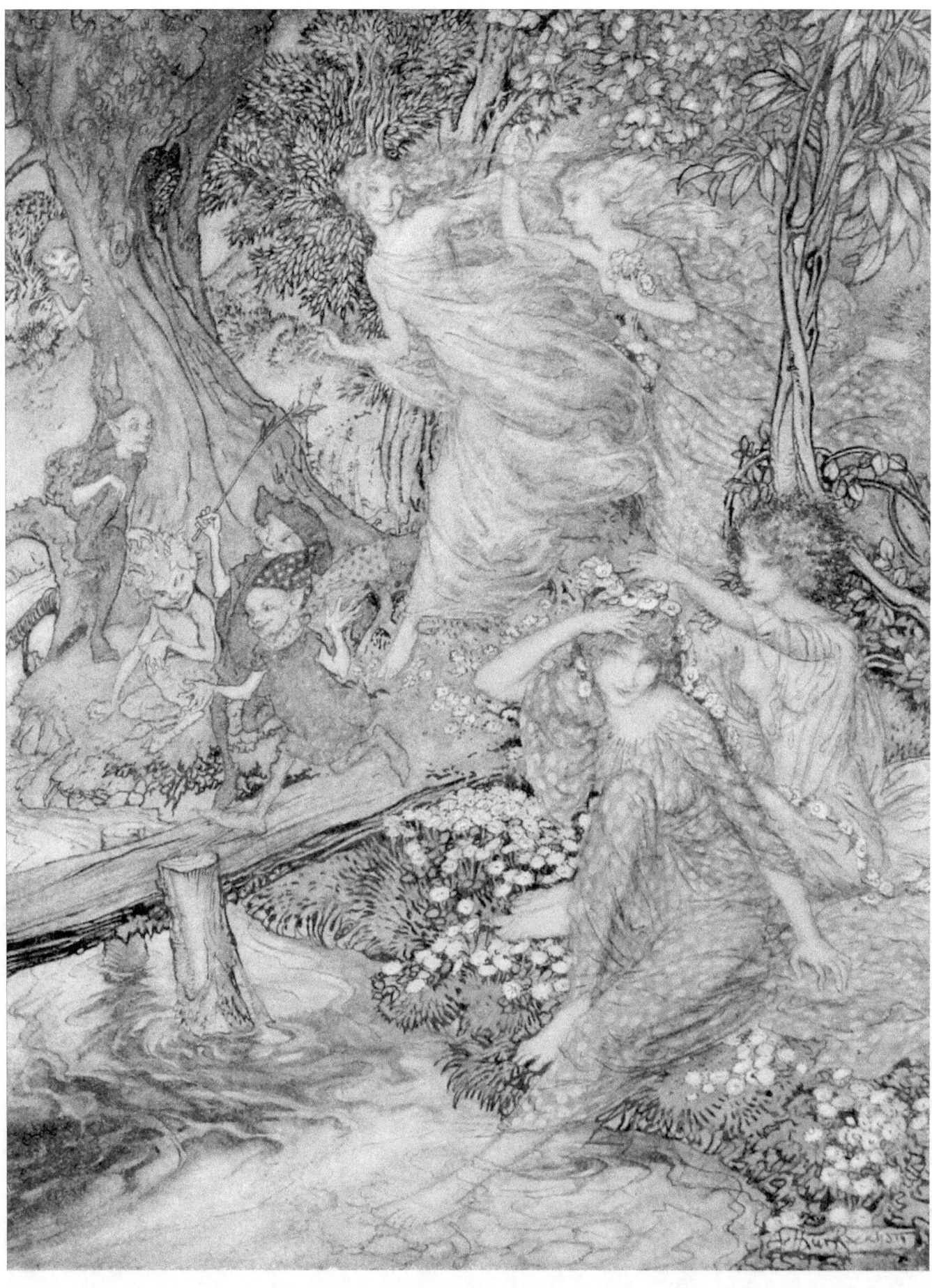

Arthur Rackham's Fairies and Nymphs

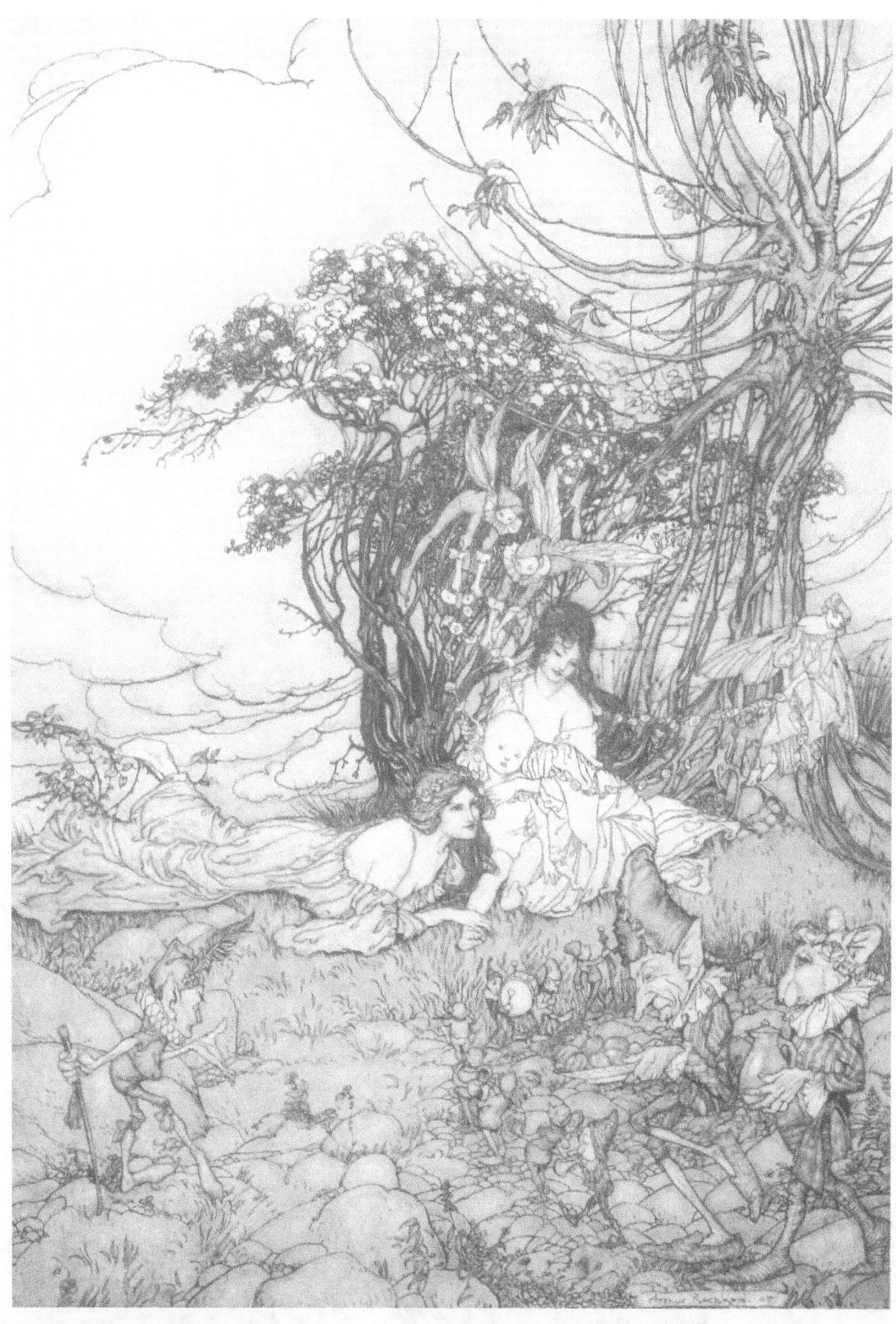

Arthur Rackham's Fairies and Nymphs

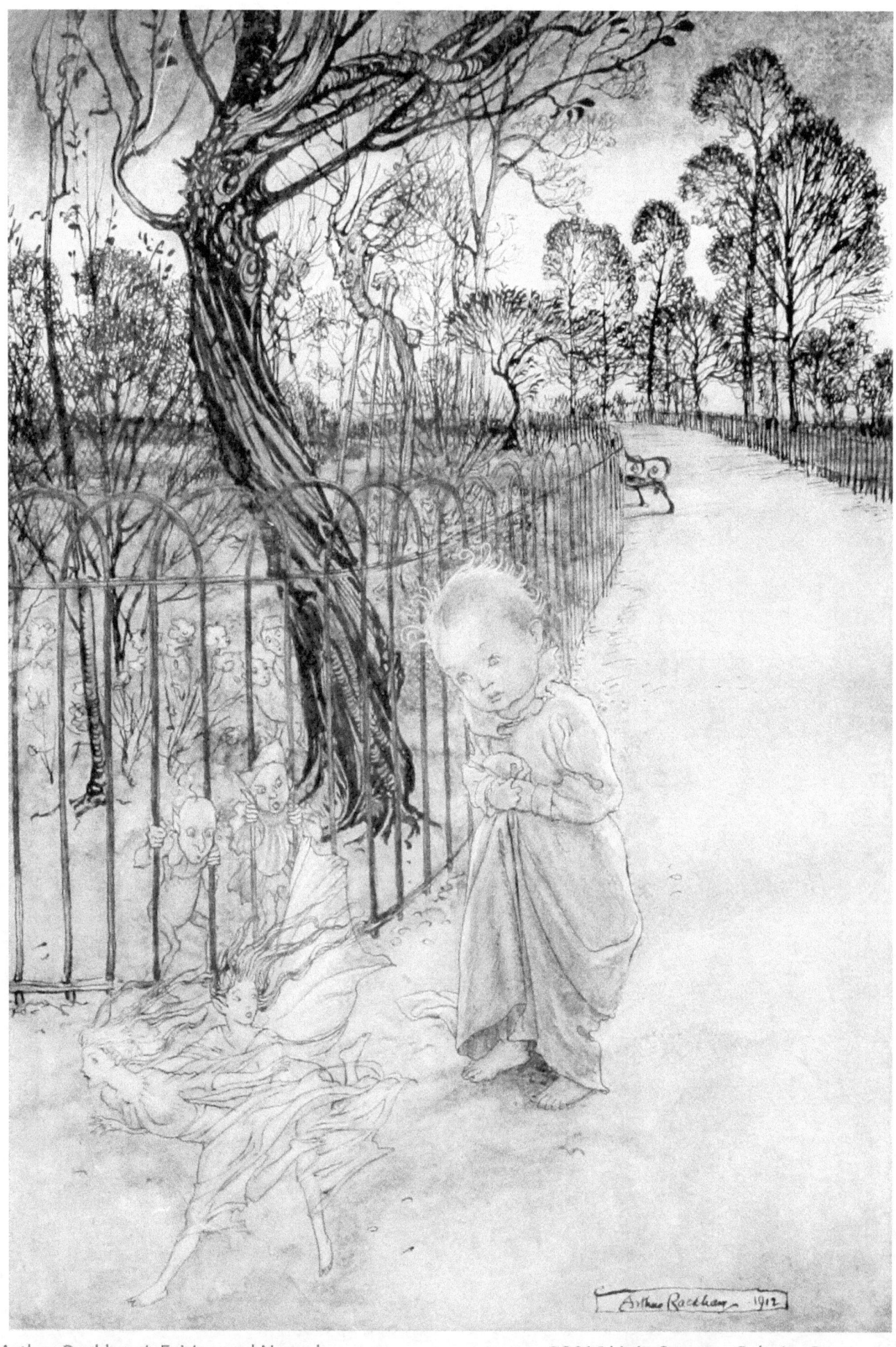

Arthur Rackham's Fairies and Nymphs

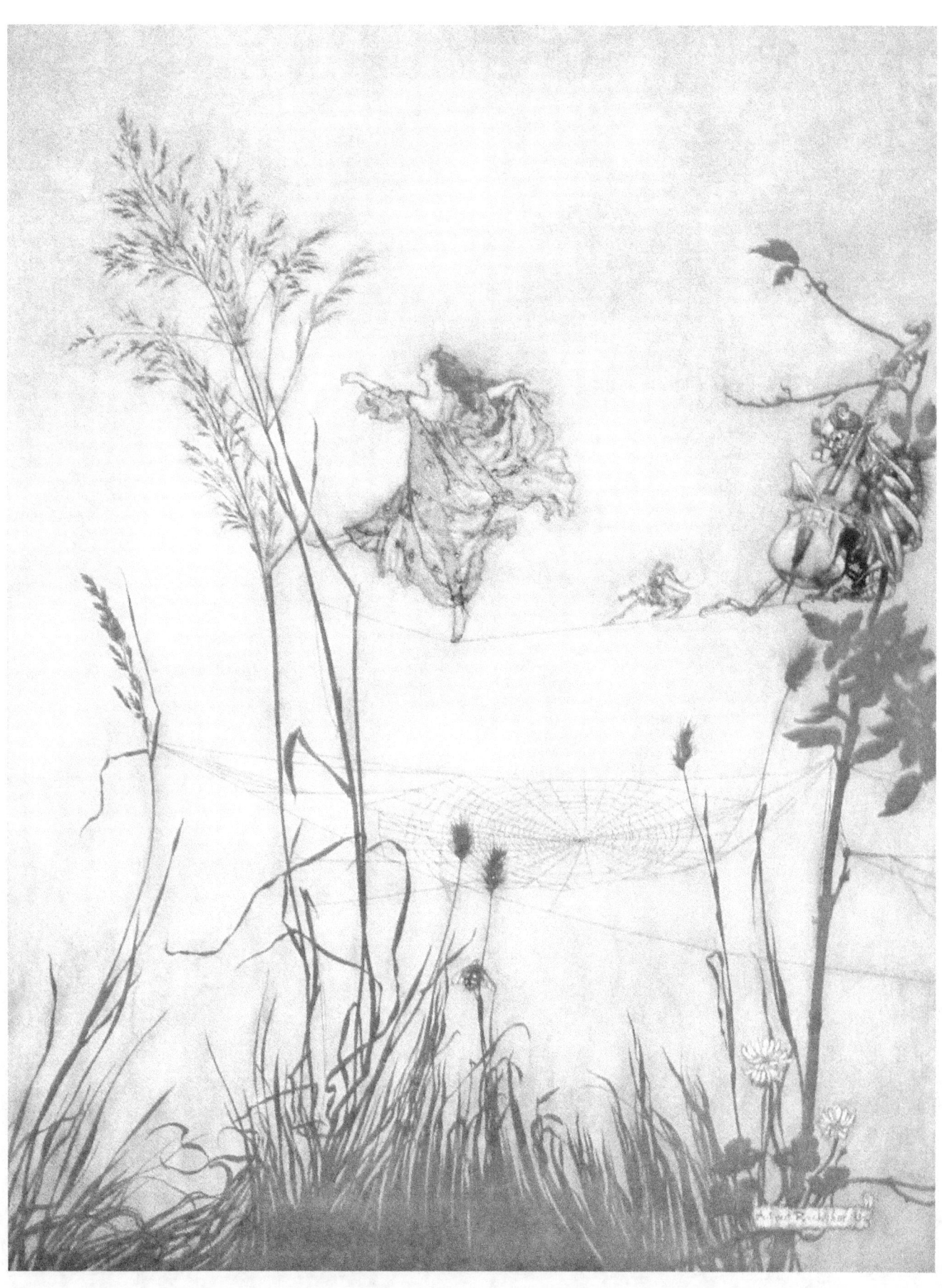

Arthur Rackham's Fairies and Nymphs

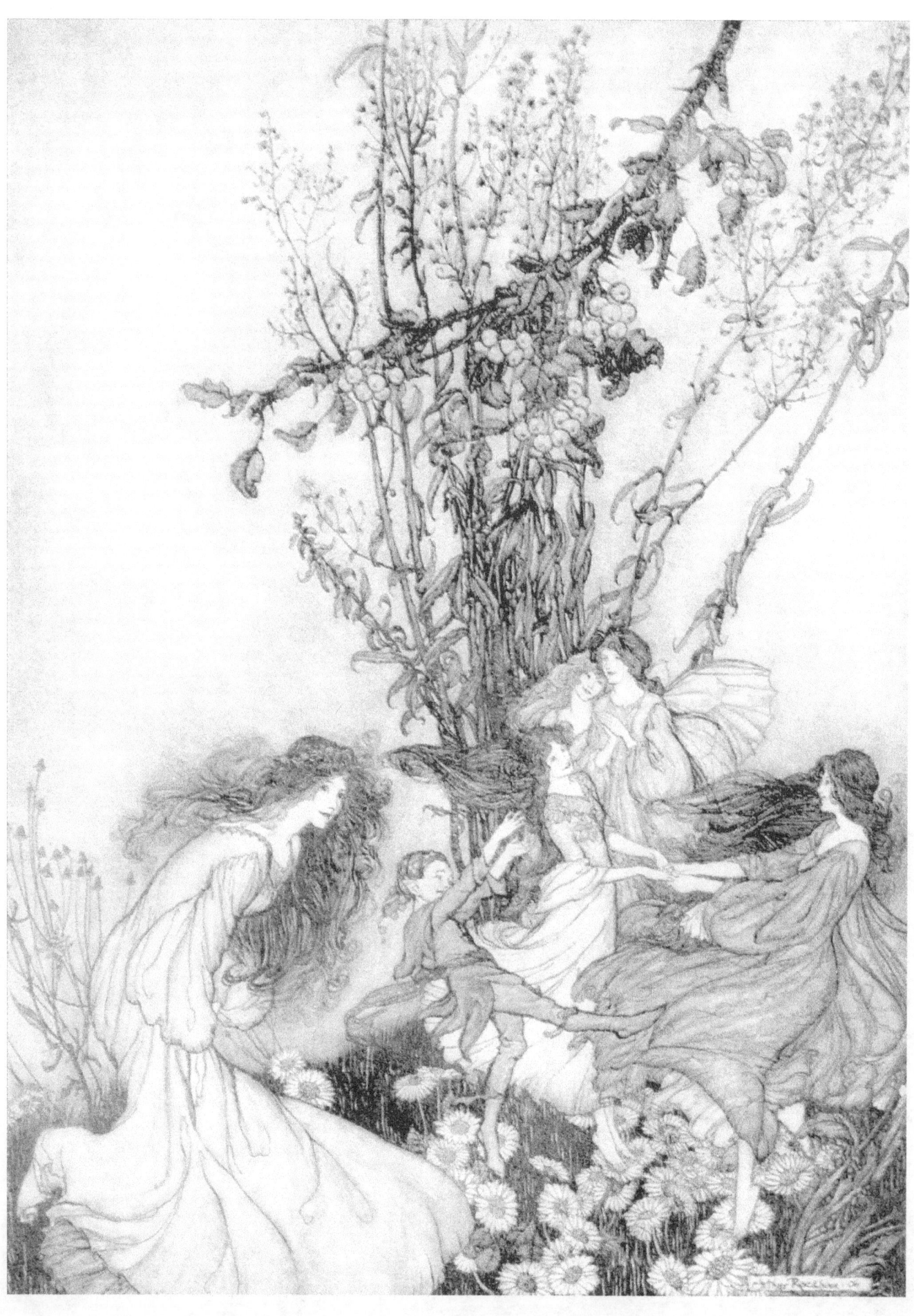

Arthur Rackham's Fairies and Nymphs

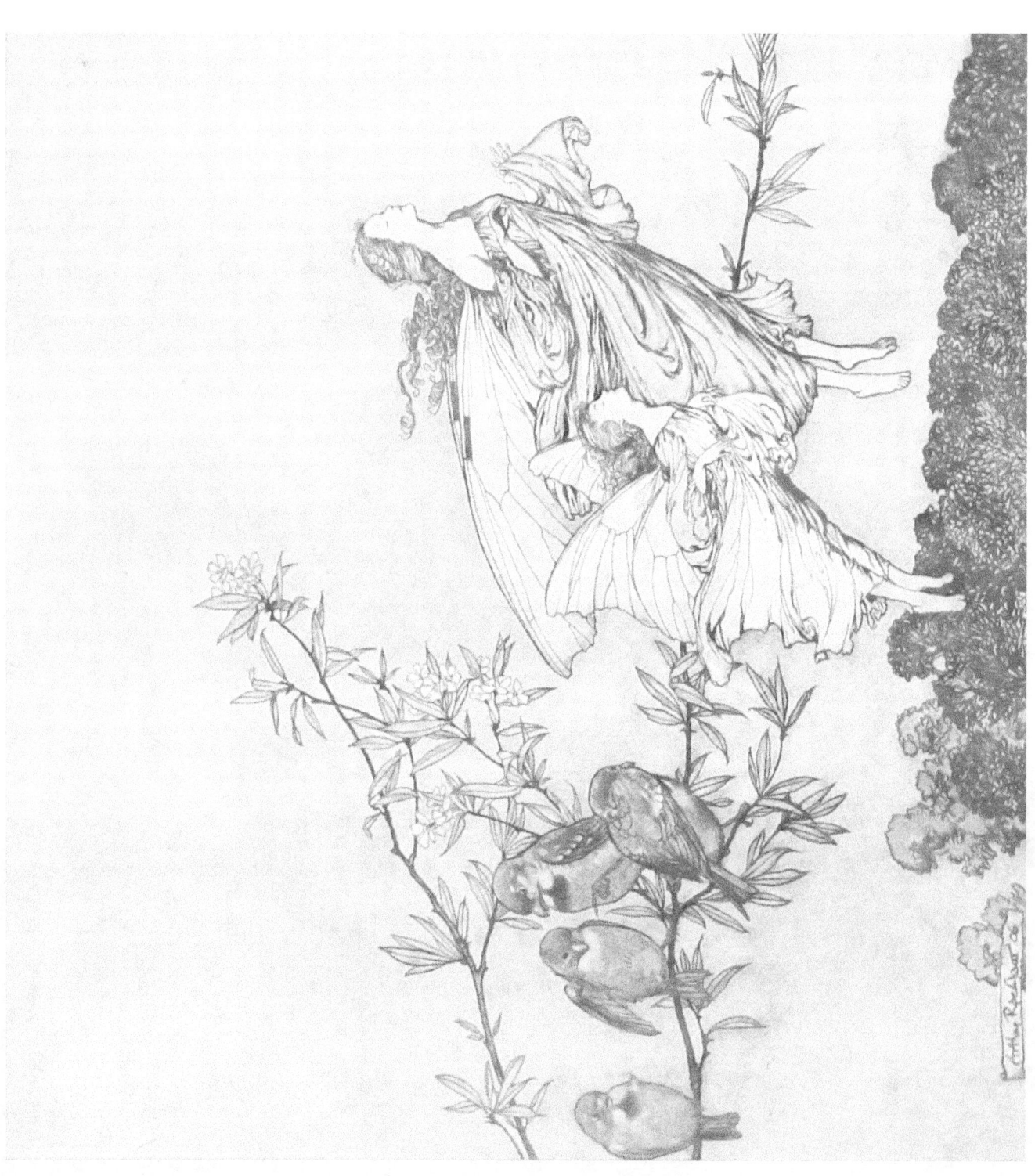

Arthur Rackham's Fairies and Nymphs

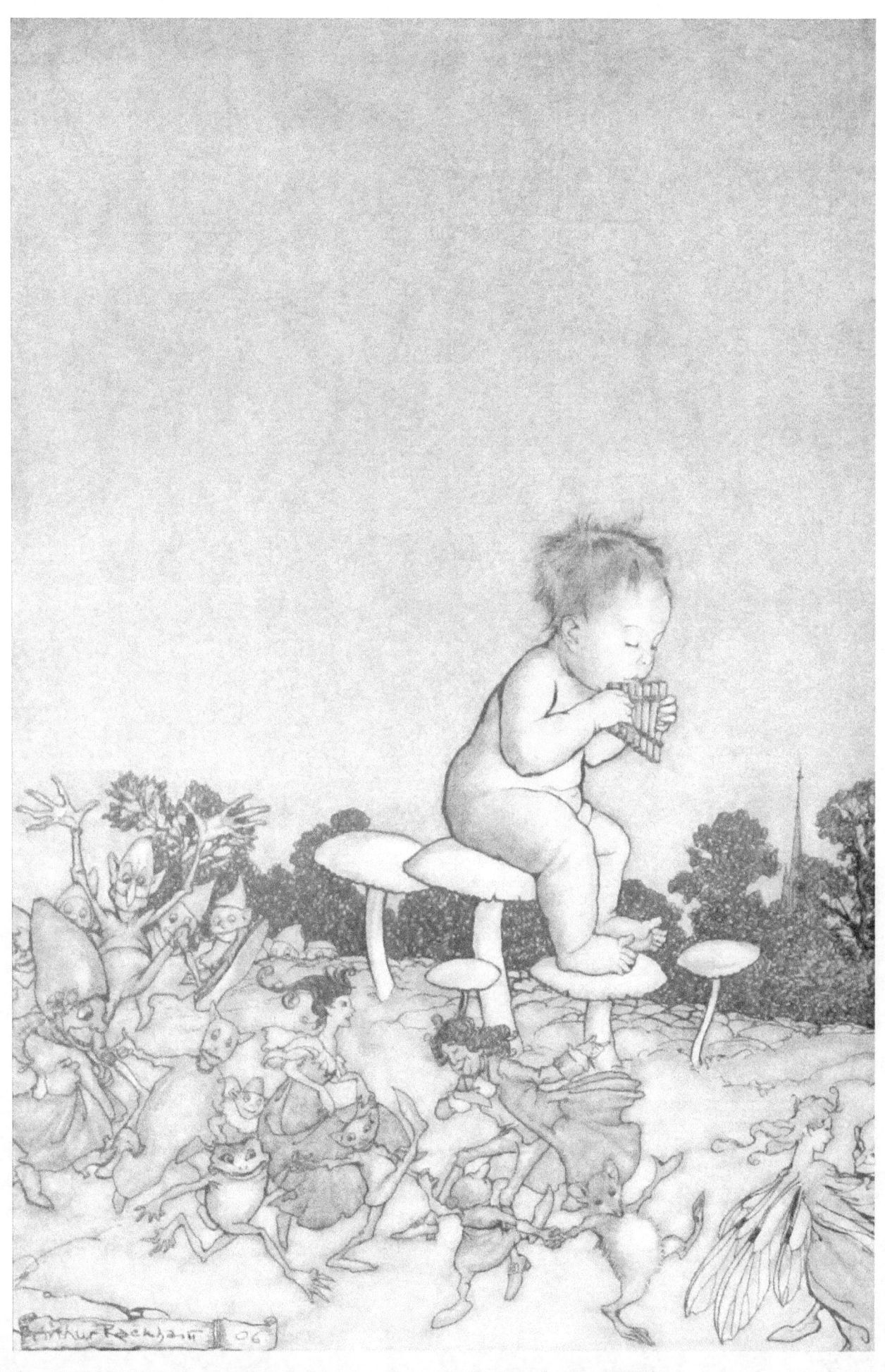

Arthur Rackham's Fairies and Nymphs

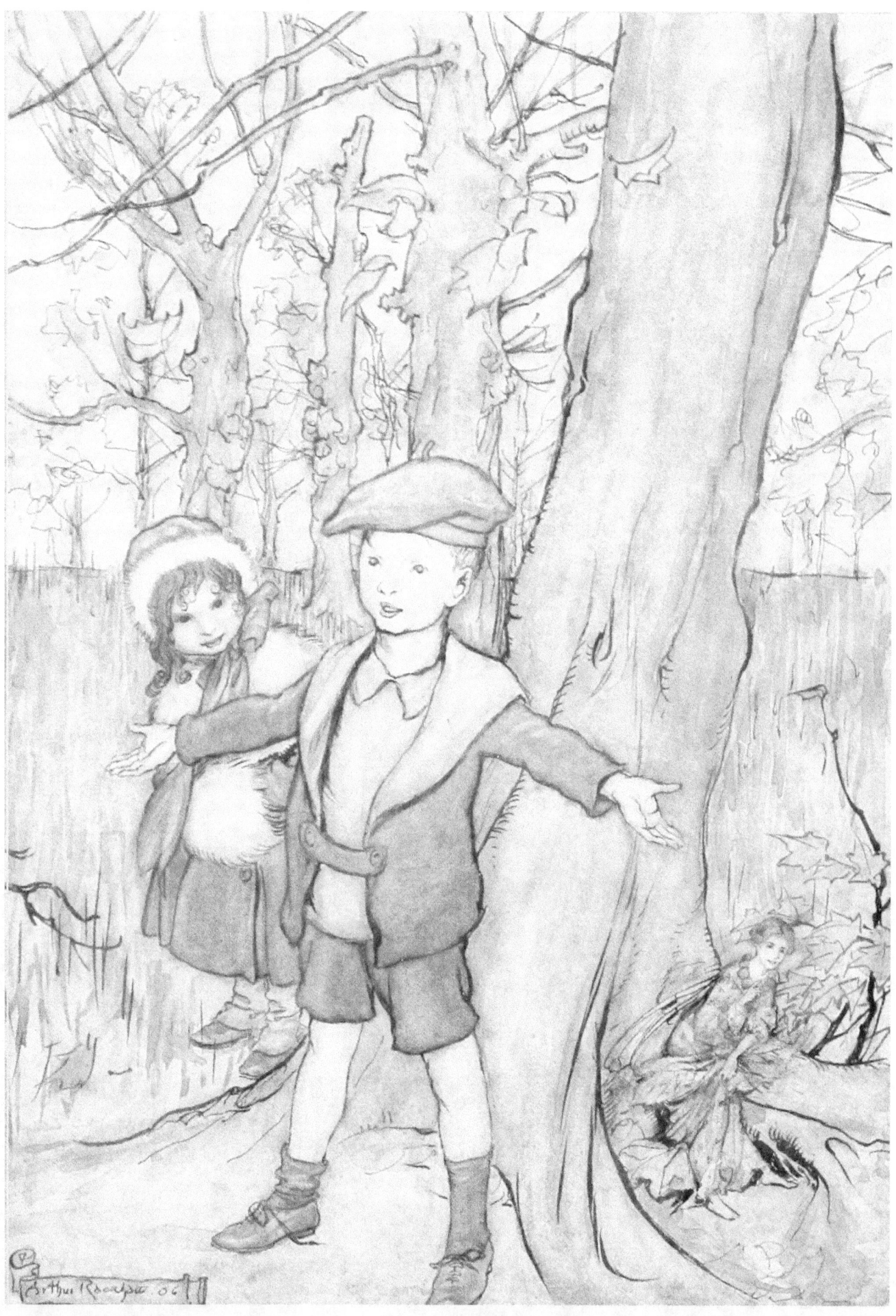

Arthur Rackham's Fairies and Nymphs

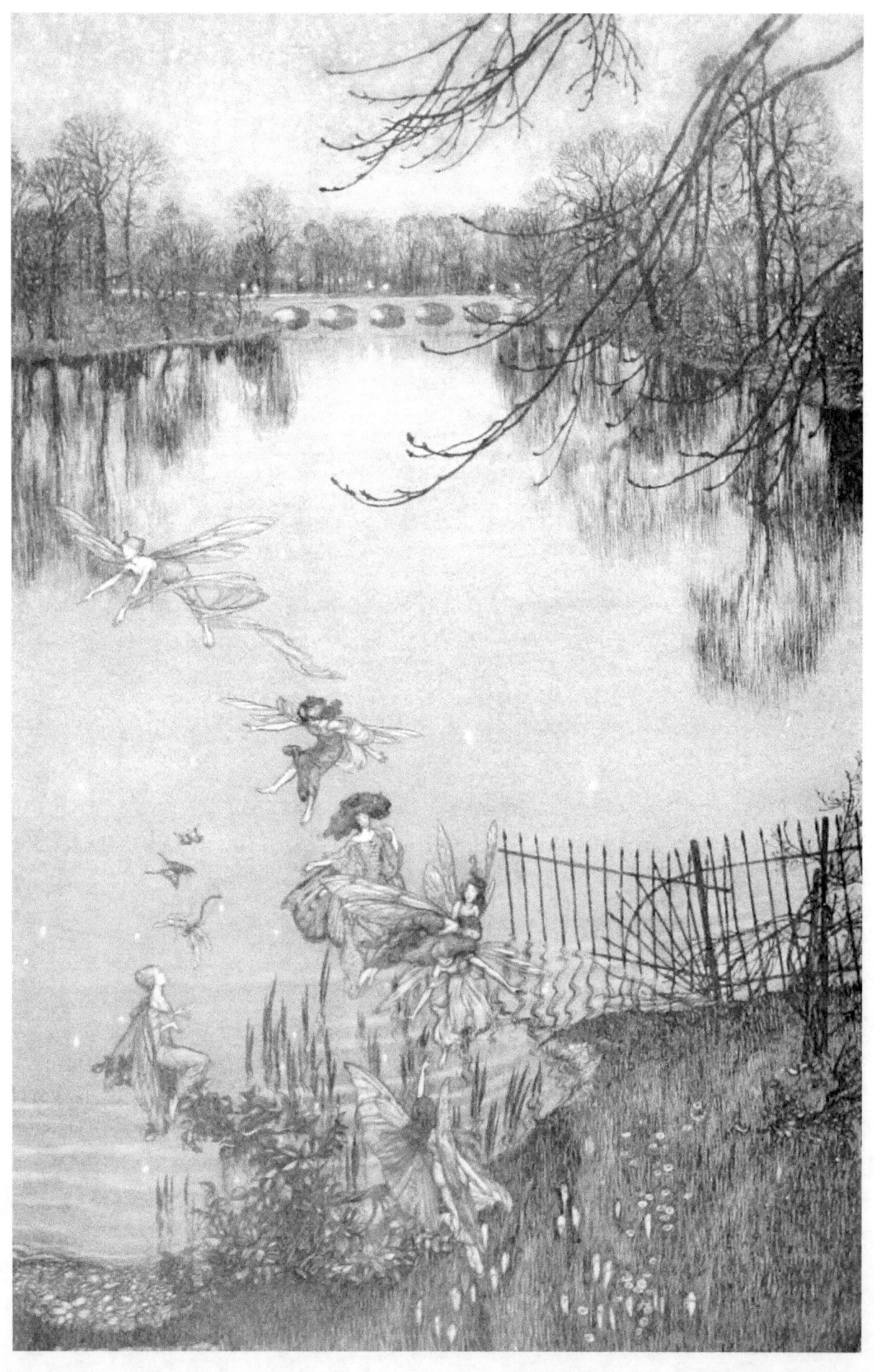

Arthur Rackham's Fairies and Nymphs

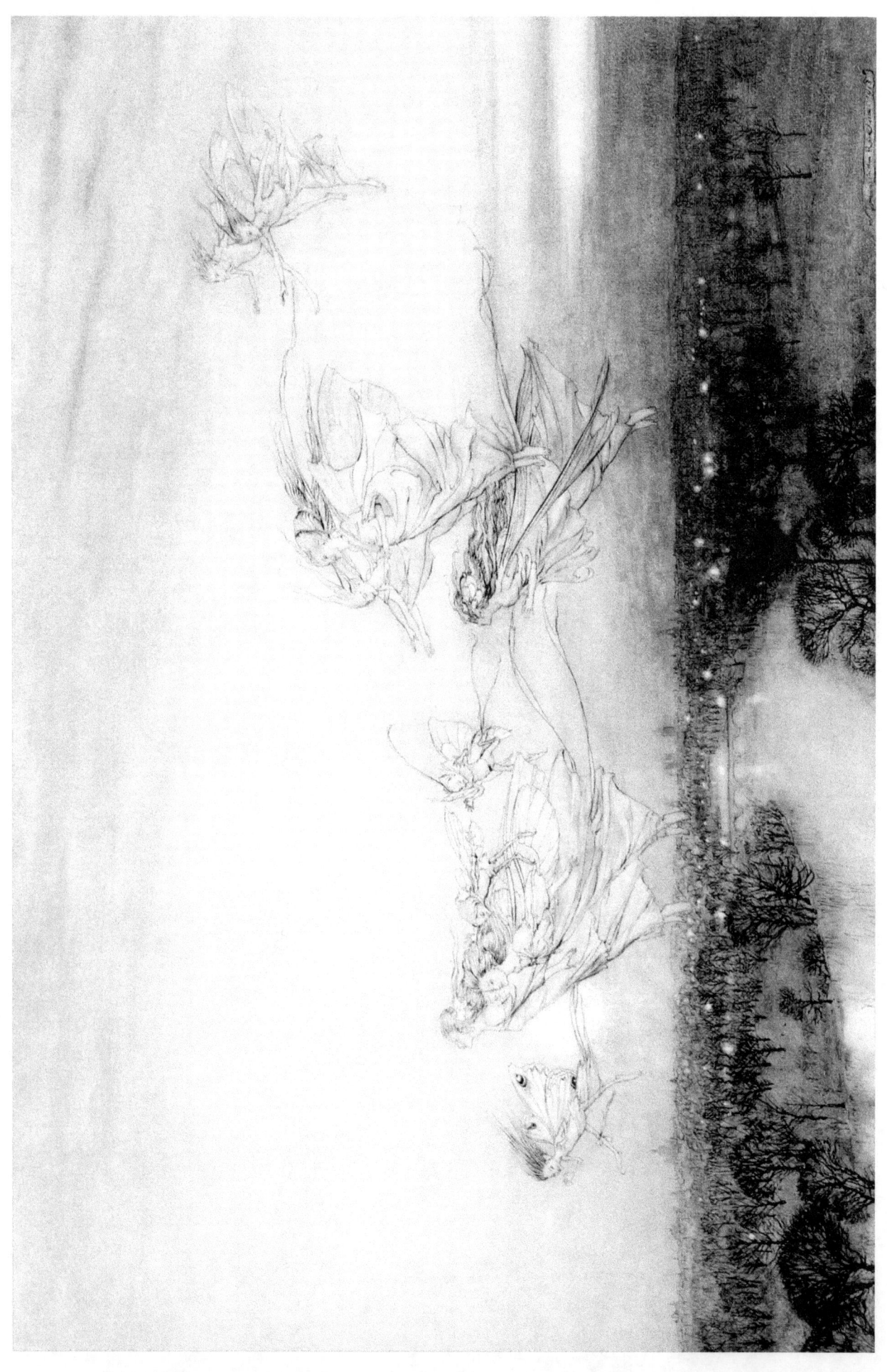

Arthur Rackham's Fairies and Nymphs

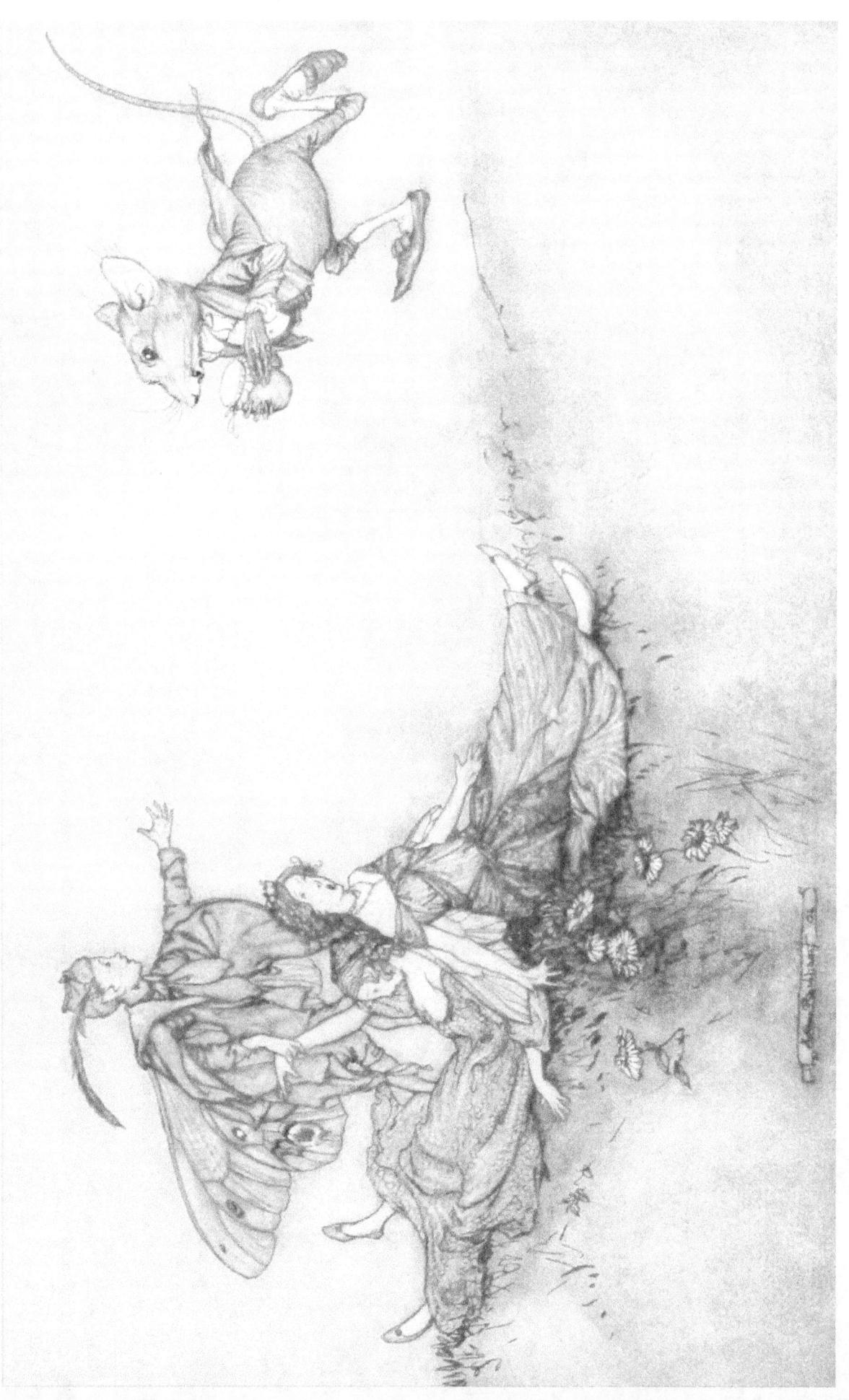

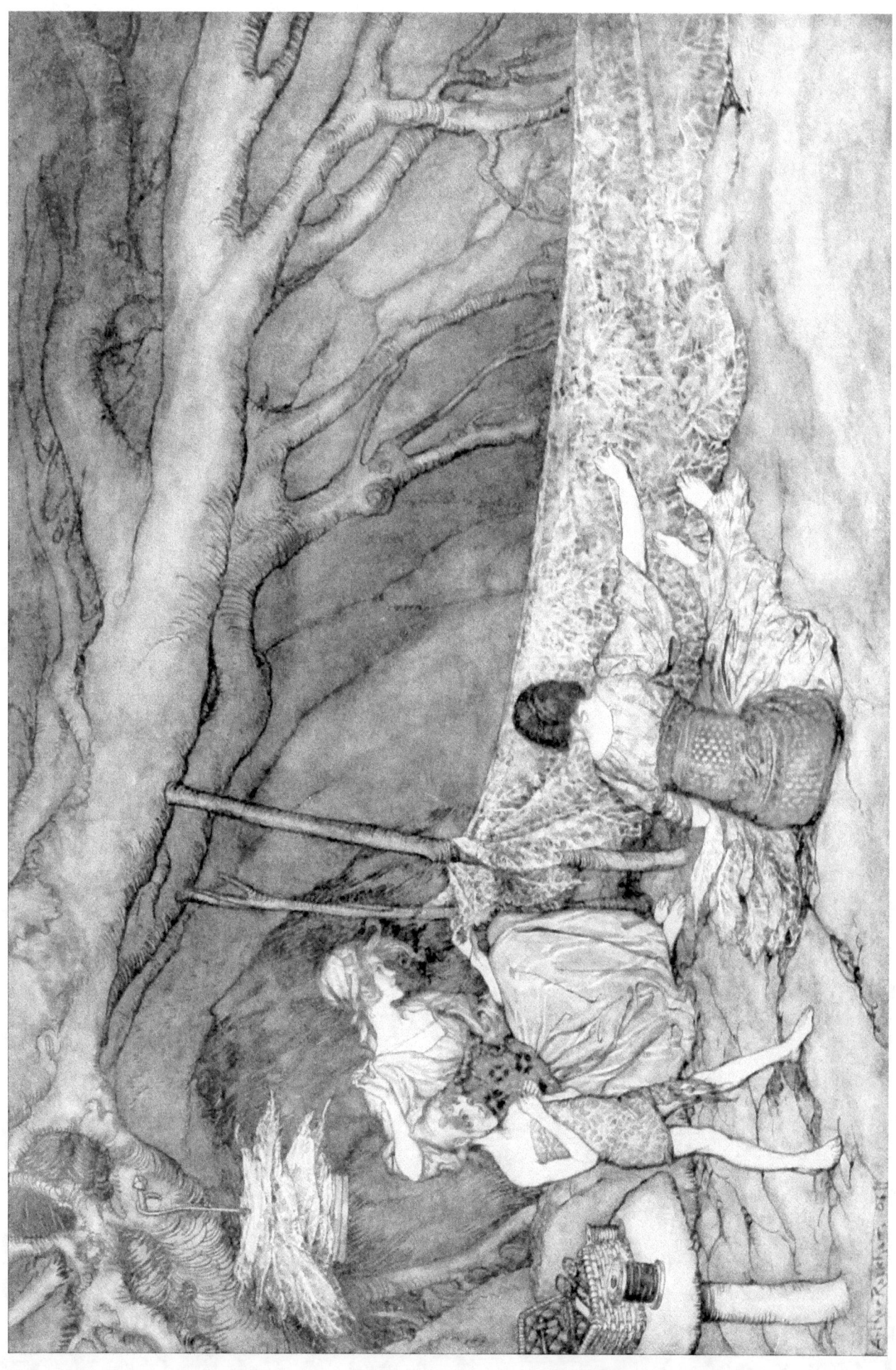

Arthur Rackham's Fairies and Nymphs   ©2016 Ligia Ortega - ColoringPress.com

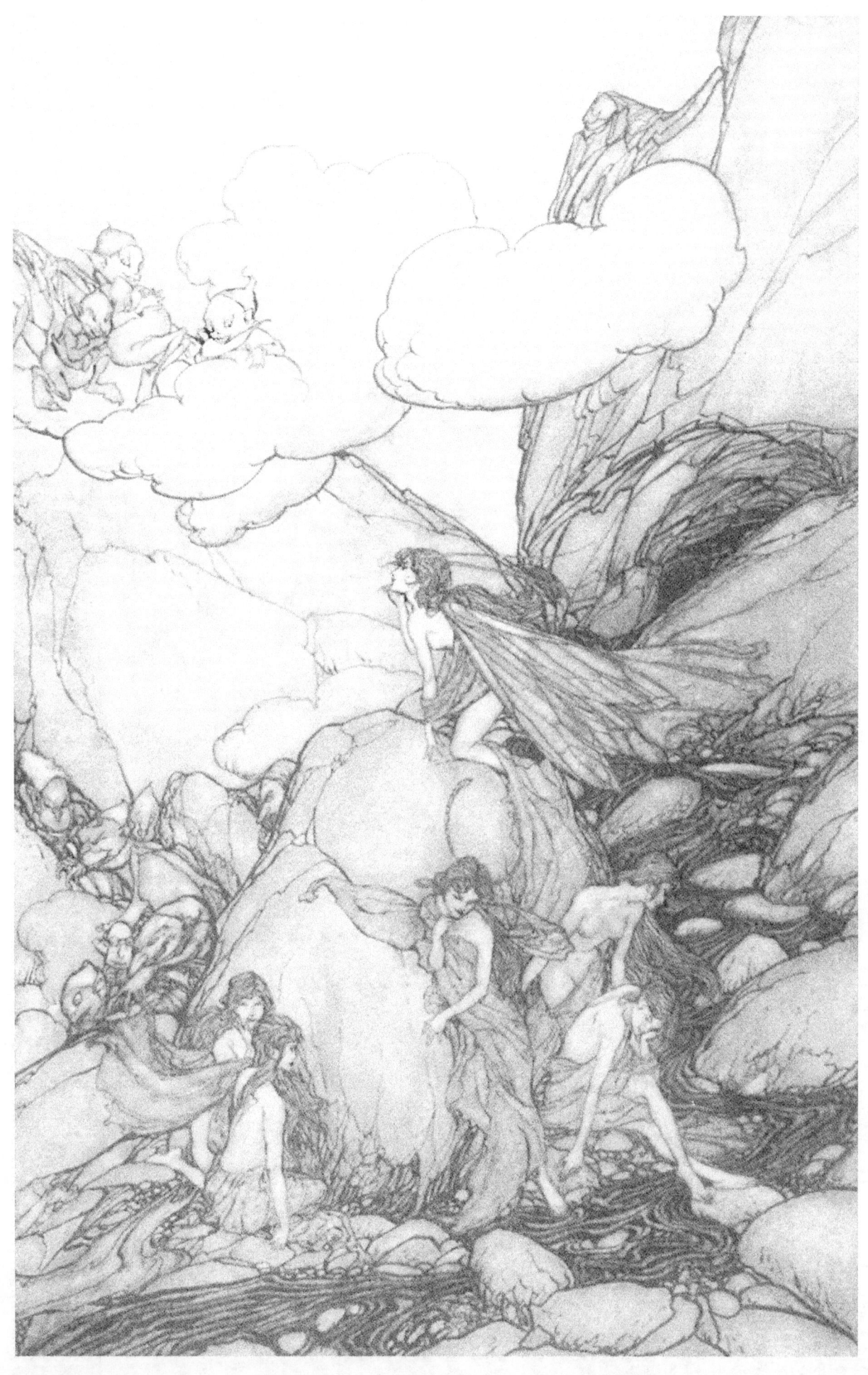

Arthur Rackham's Fairies and Nymphs   ©2016 Ligia Ortega - ColoringPress.com

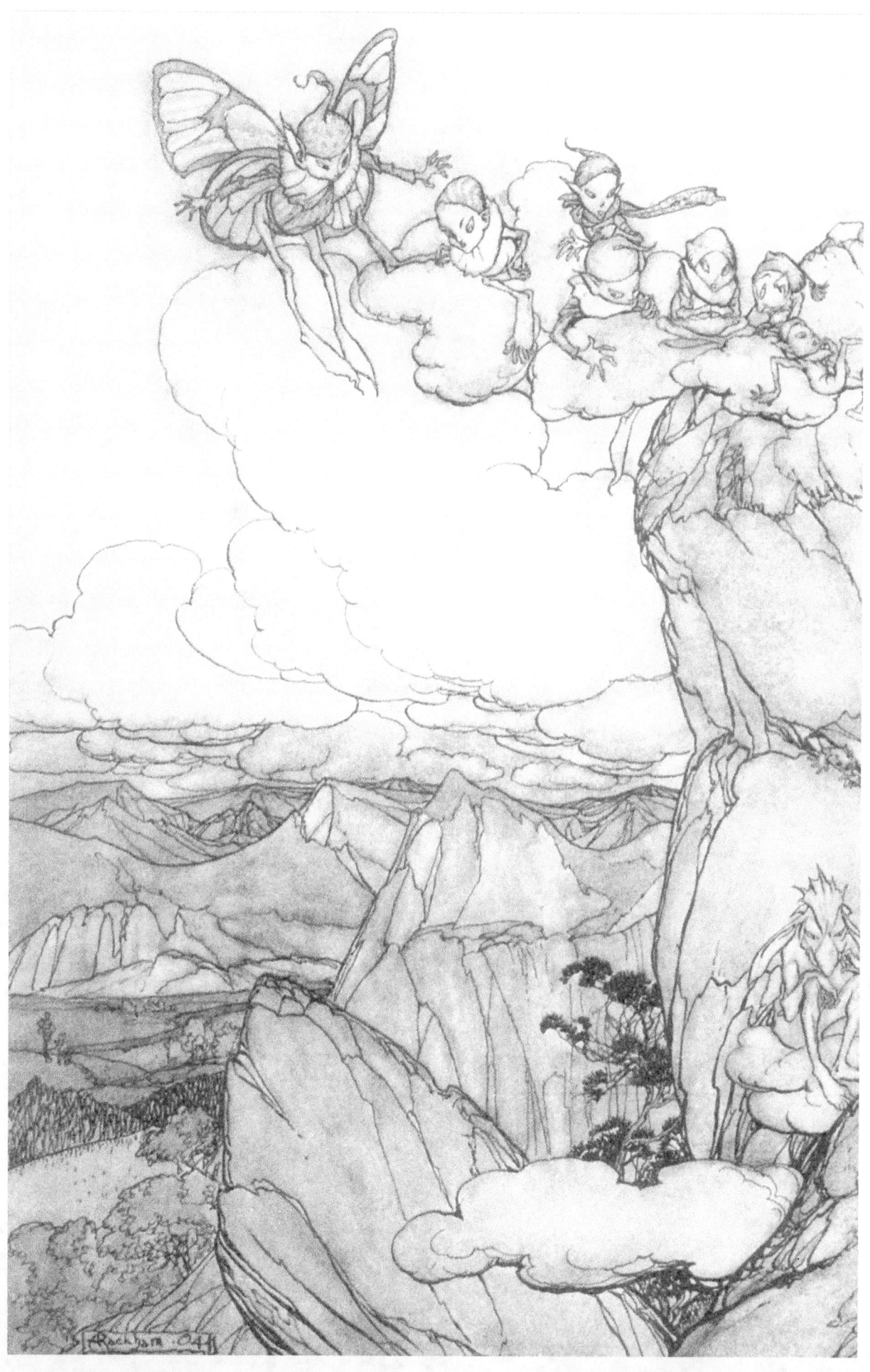

Arthur Rackham's Fairies and Nymphs

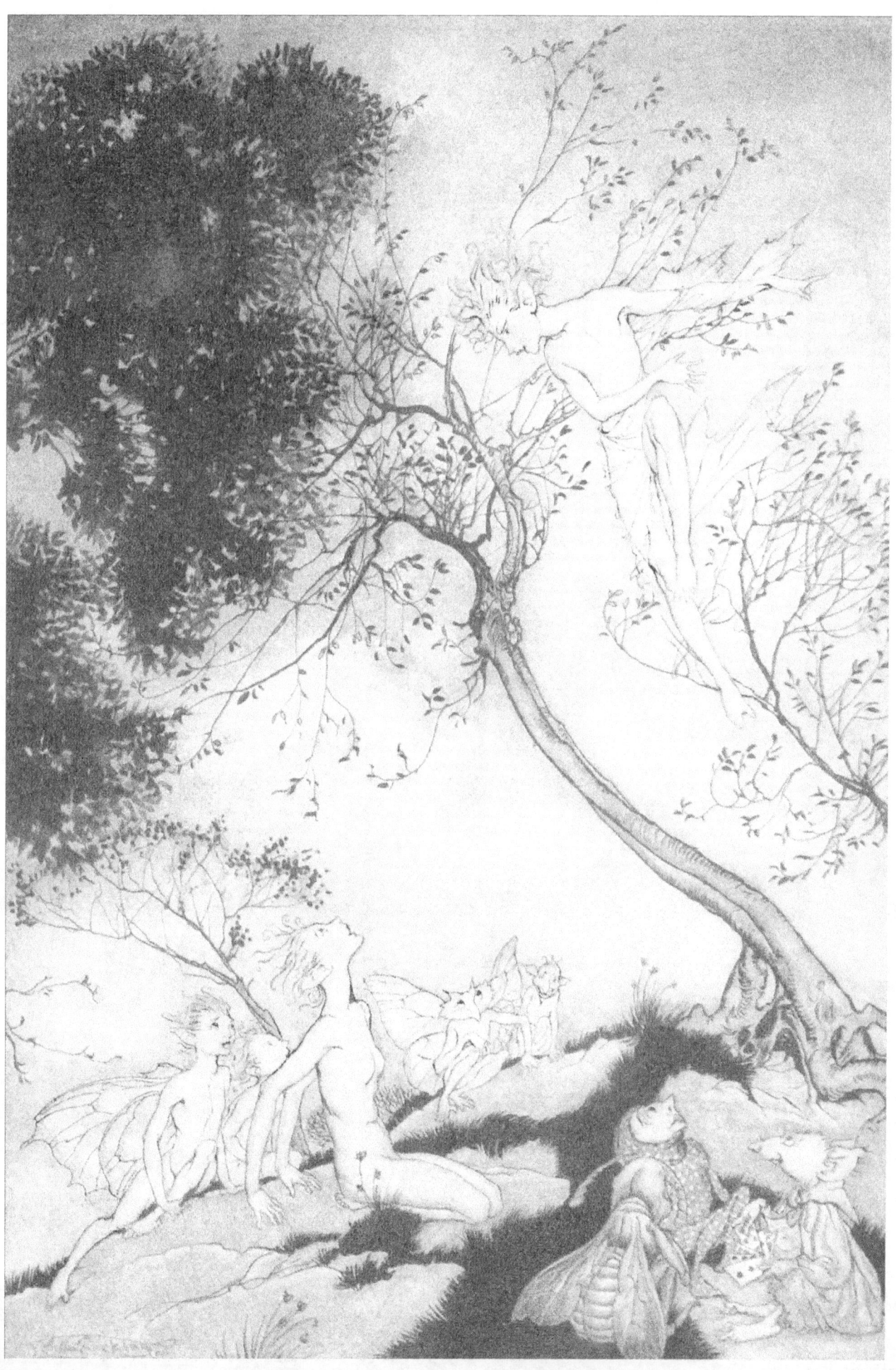

Arthur Rackham's Fairies and Nymphs

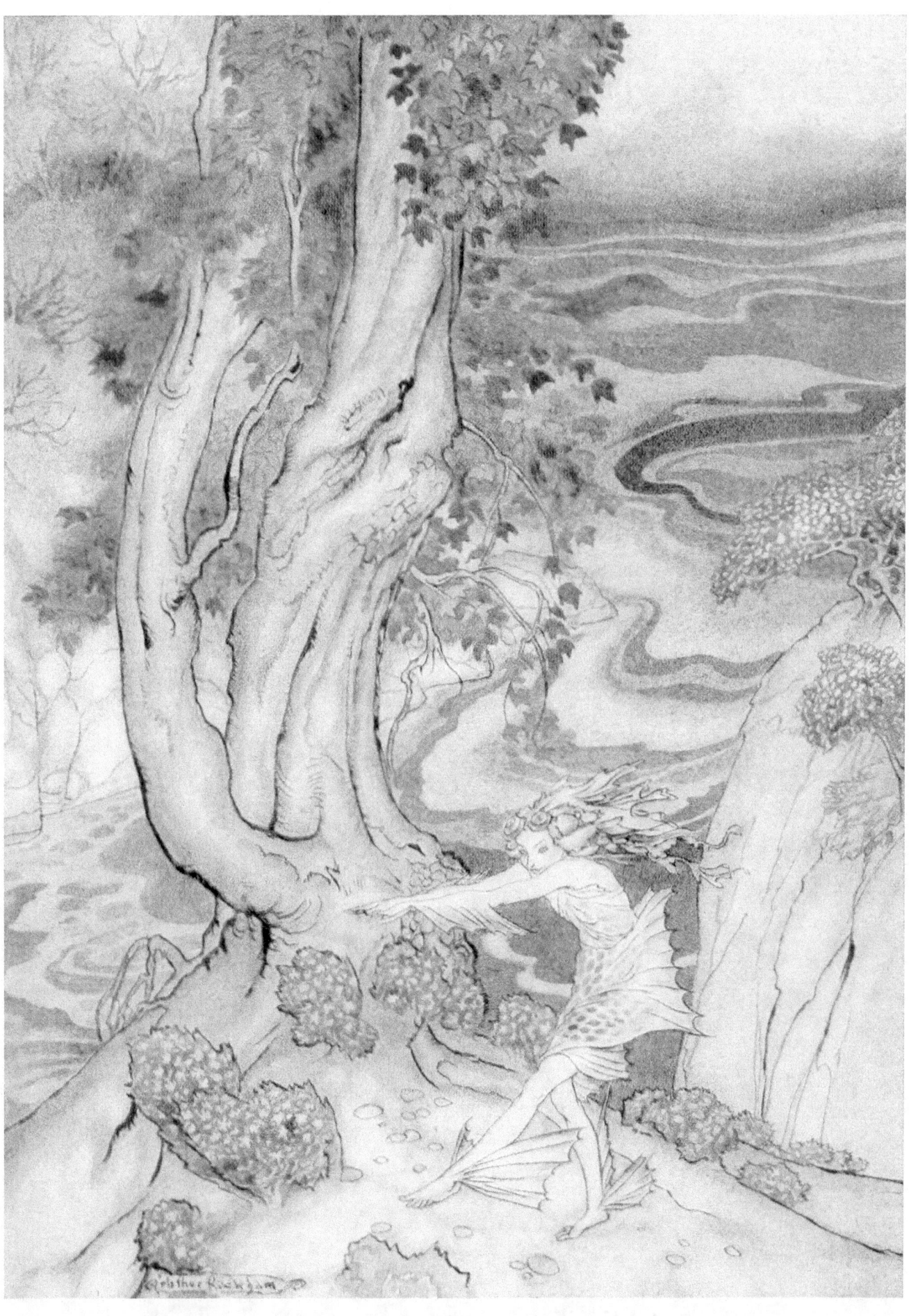

Arthur Rackham's Fairies and Nymphs

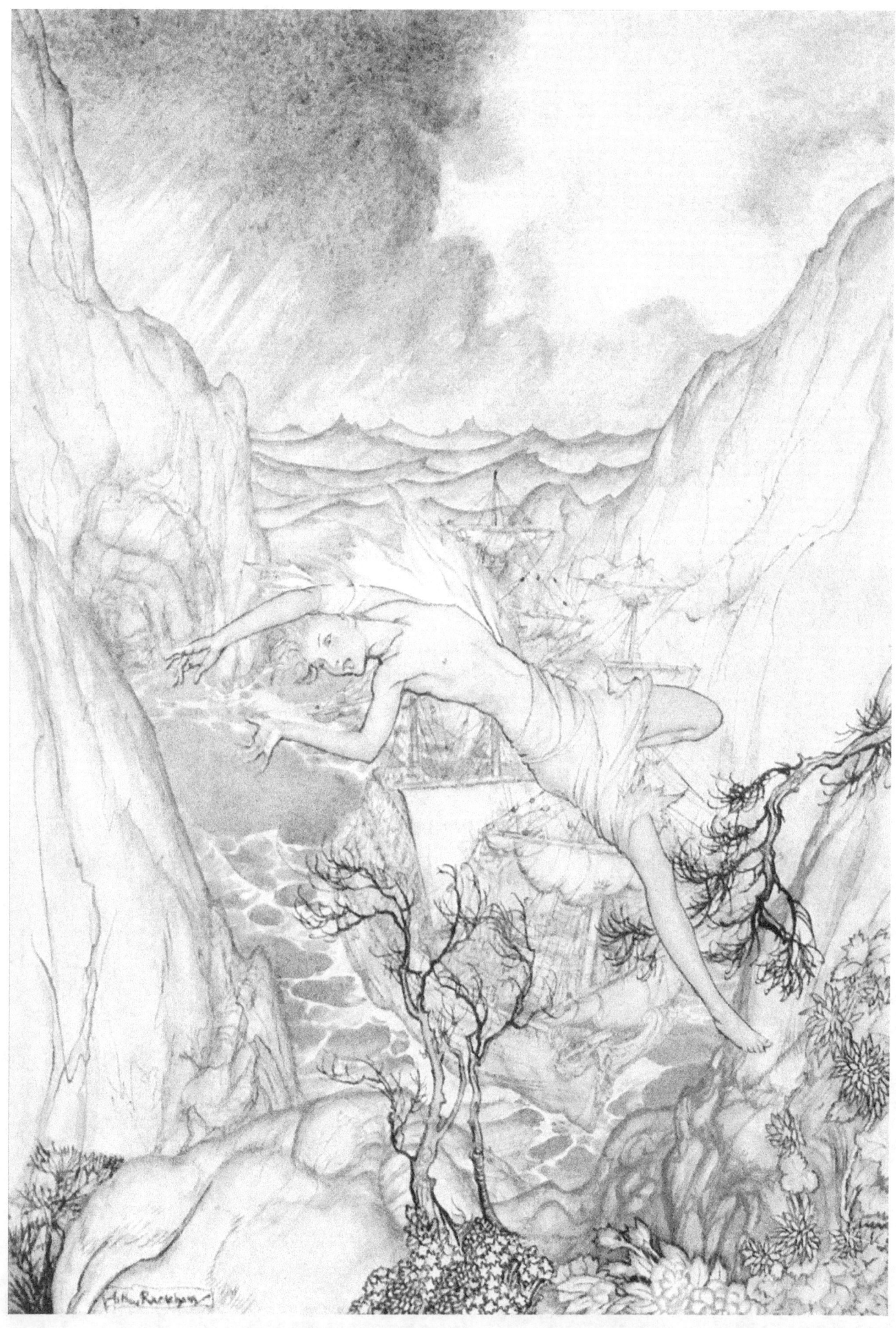

Arthur Rackham's Fairies and Nymphs

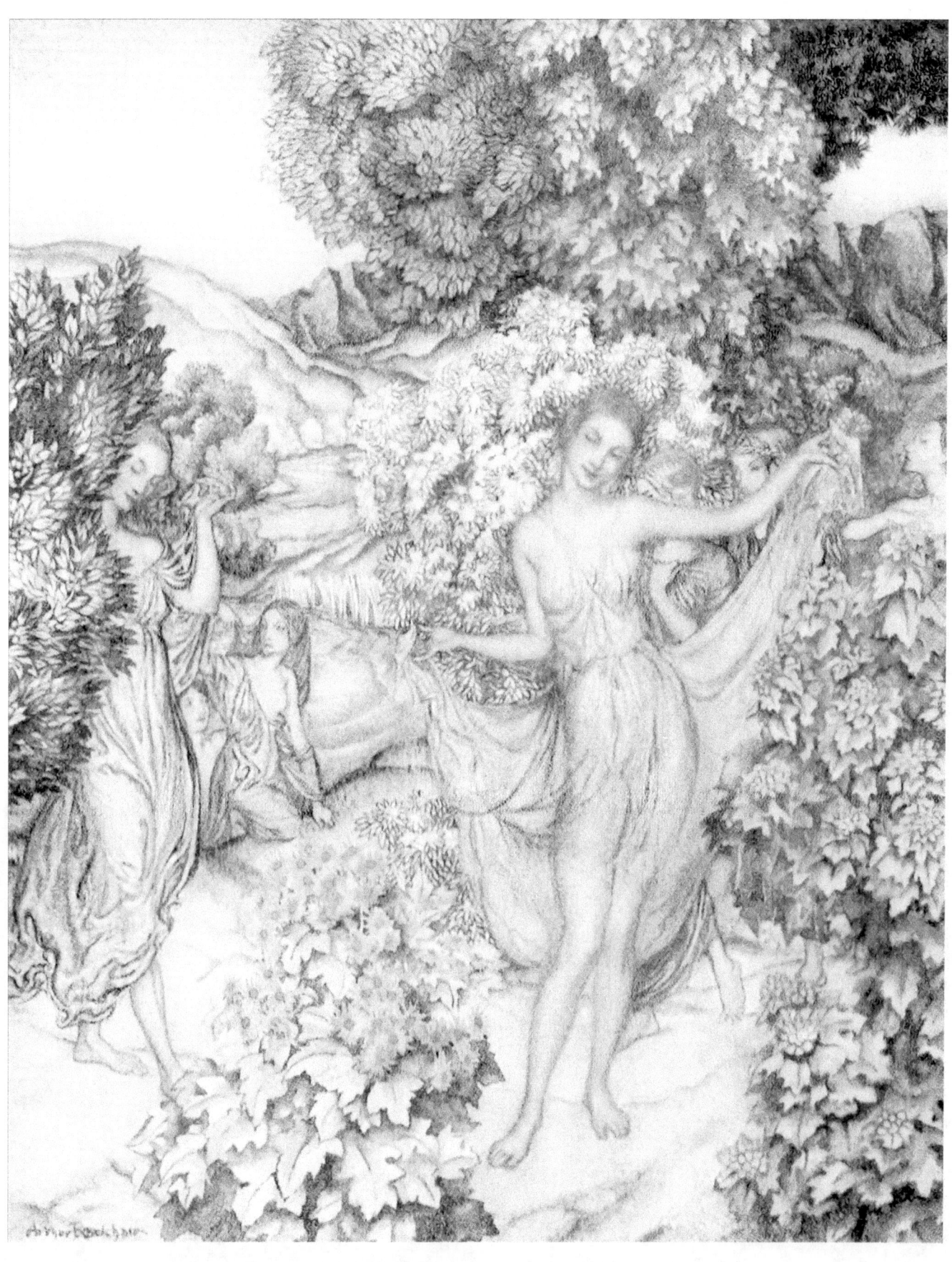

Arthur Rackham's Fairies and Nymphs

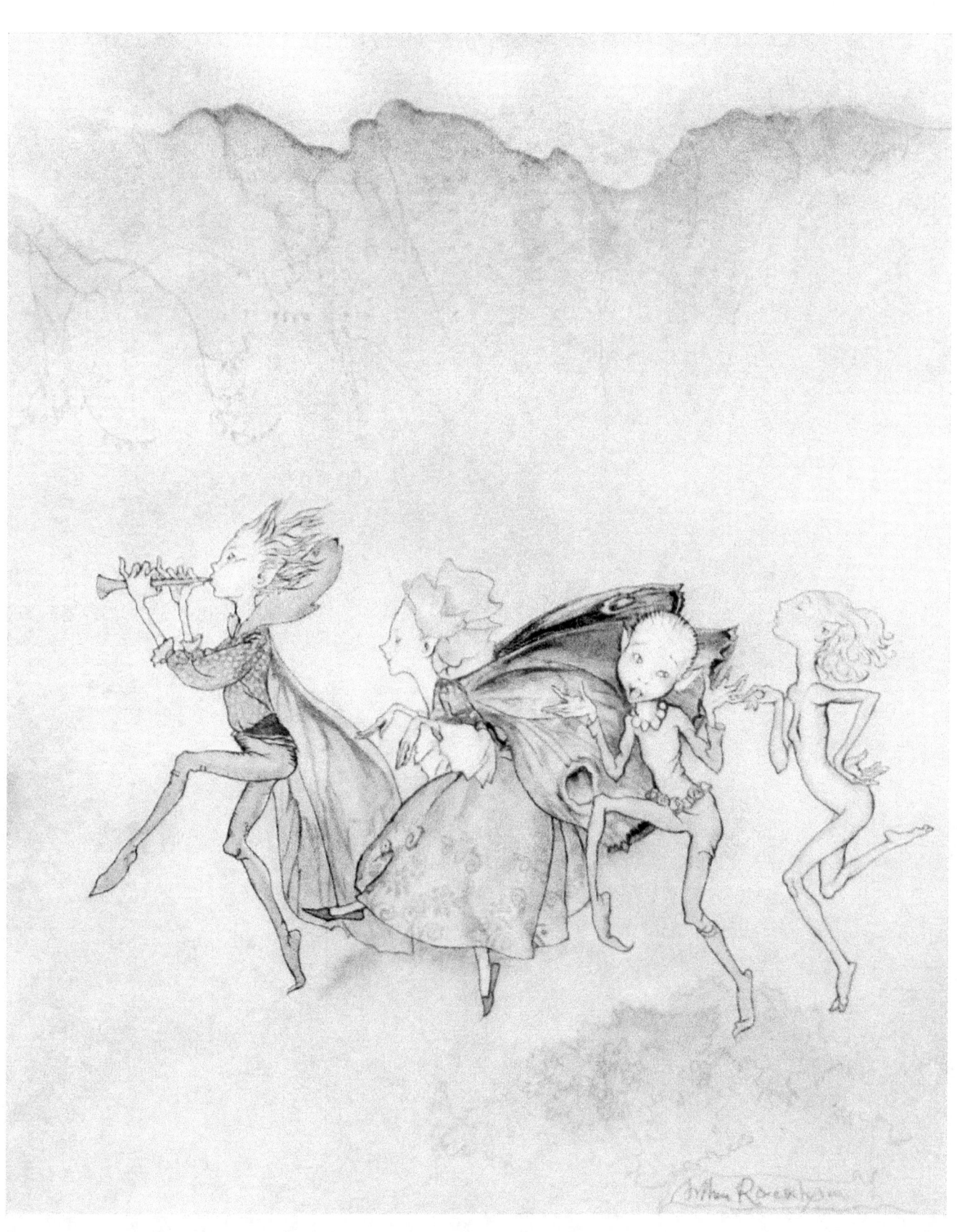

Arthur Rackham's Fairies and Nymphs   ©2016 Ligia Ortega - ColoringPress.com

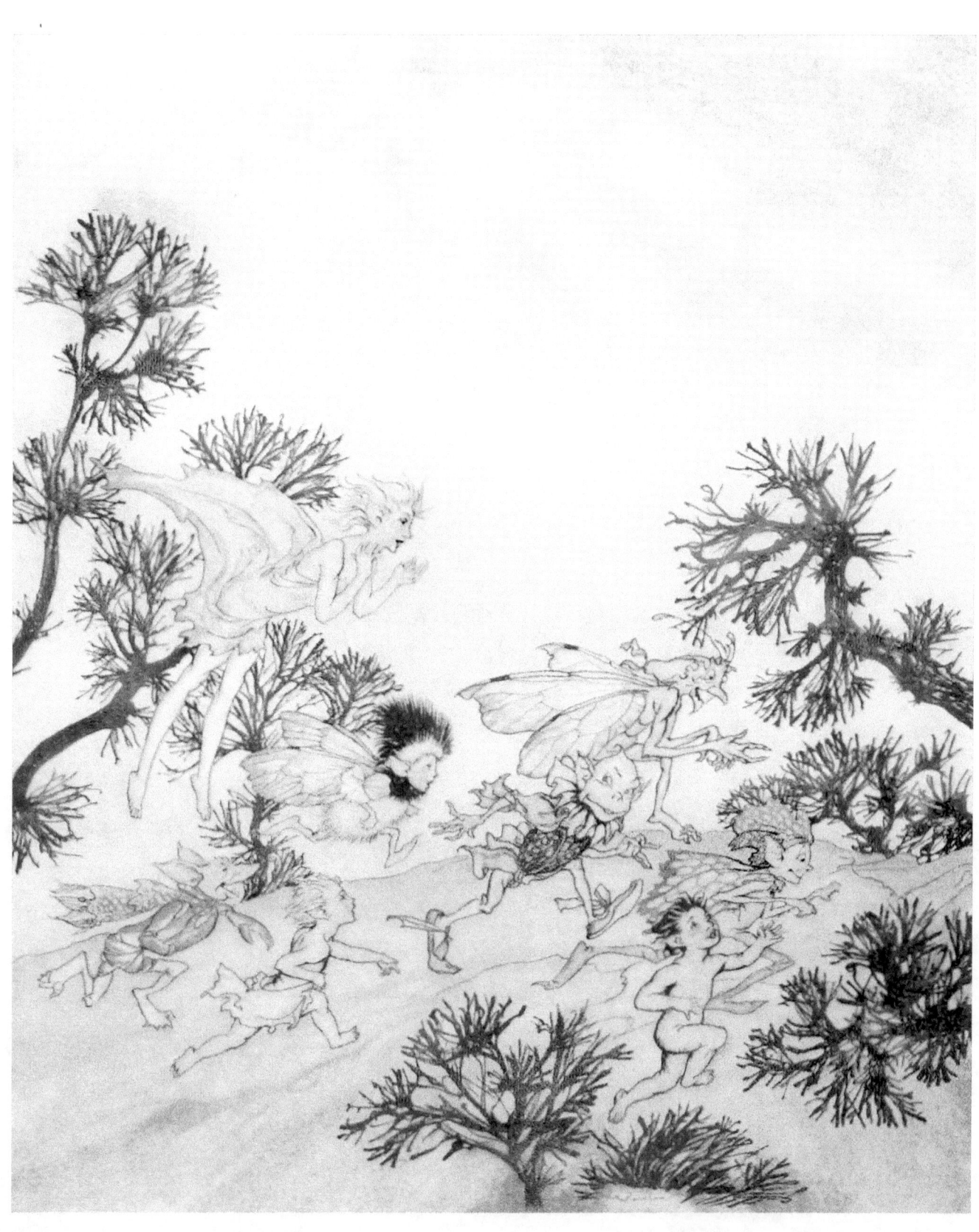

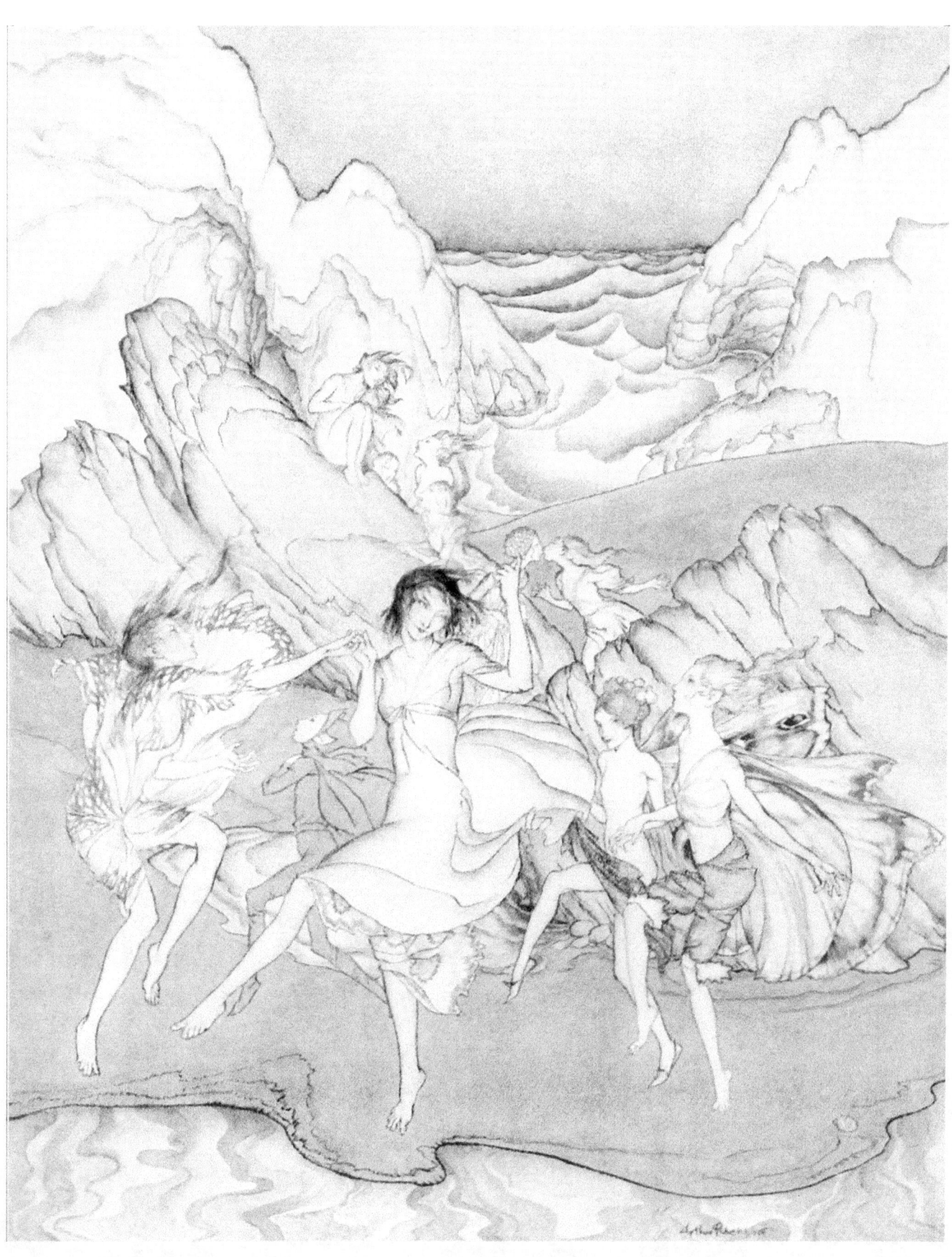

Arthur Rackham's Fairies and Nymphs

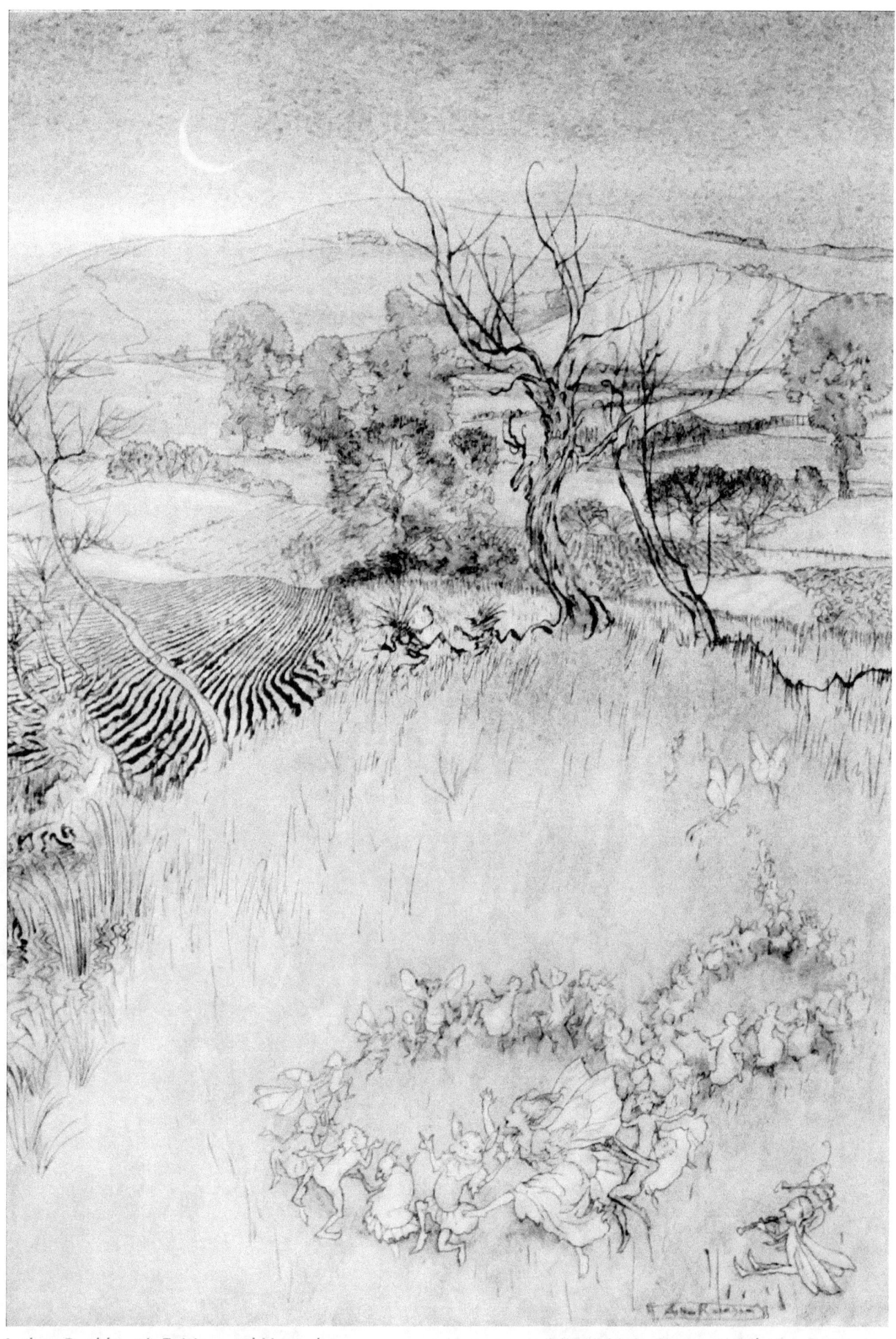

Arthur Rackham's Fairies and Nymphs   ©2016 Ligia Ortega - ColoringPress.com

BONUS PAGES

In addition to the *Vintage Grayscale Adult Coloring Book* series, I have been working on other coloring books for adults. The following coloring pages are from books I have published under Coloring Press.

The first image is a sample from Volume 1 of my *Coloring Gifts™* Book Series, *Coloring Gifts™: Gifts of Thanks*. This gratitude-themed adult coloring book has 24 original hand drawn pages printed in two different sizes plus nine bookmarks that can be colored and given as is, or framed, turned into cards, or made into bookmarks using the included instructions. These pages can also be used to aid prayer or meditation to reap the full health benefits of gratitude. I am already working on the second volume of *Coloring Gifts™: Gifts of Encouragement*. This next book is full size 8.5x11" will offer caring and support to loved ones going through life's difficulties. Visit ColoringPress.com for more information on *Coloring Gifts™*.

The remaining images are from my *Simple Kaleidoscopes* coloring books. I took on the challenge of making kaleidoscope images by hand rather than having software generated ones. I used old-fashioned math to measure angles and calculate what needed to be done to cut, duplicate, and rotate my source image to make these kaleidoscopes. It was fun watching them come to life from my own hand-drawn black and white coloring image. These kaleidoscopes are published as full size 8.5x11" books and also as travel size 6x8" books both in regular and black background versions. I am publishing these full size kaleidoscope books in response to many colorists asking for a less intricate kaleidoscope where they could show off their shading or just have larger spaces to color. The travel size books are perfect for taking with you to the mechanic, the dentist, the doctor's office, or any place where you may have to wait. They truly make the time fly by quickly and the wait a lot more pleasant, and their small size means you can usually finish coloring a page in one sitting.

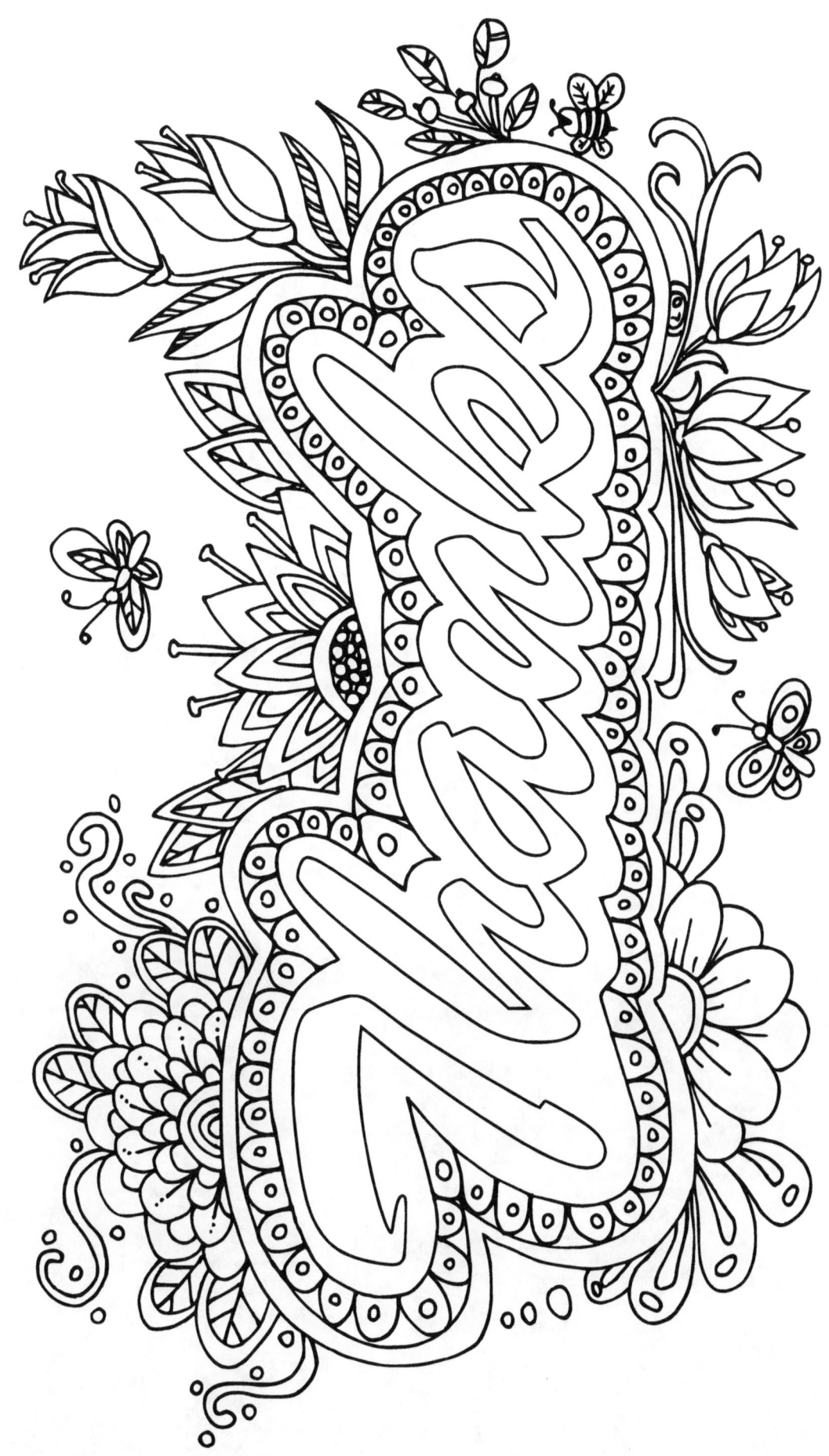

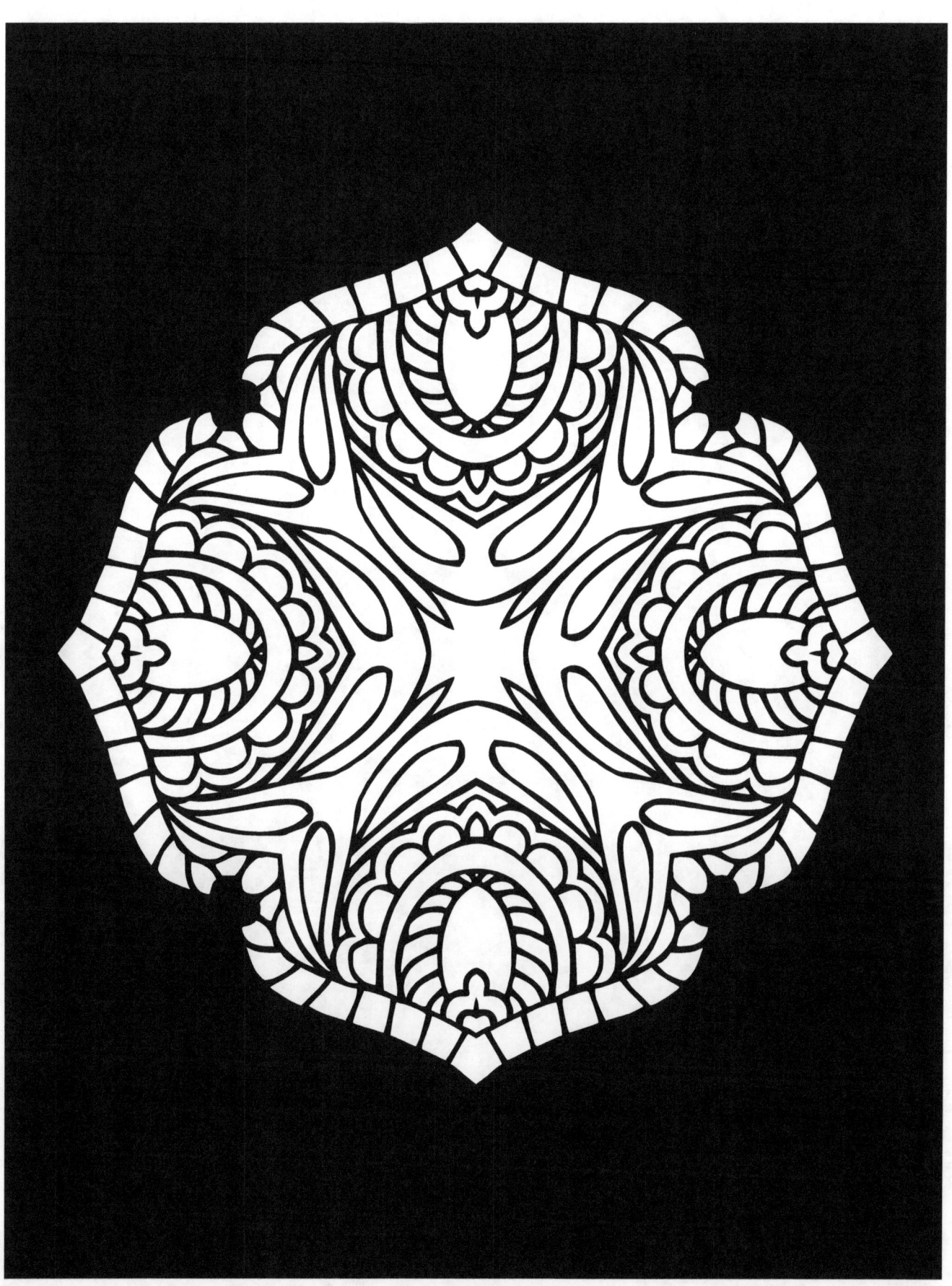

Simple Kaleidoscopes Black Background

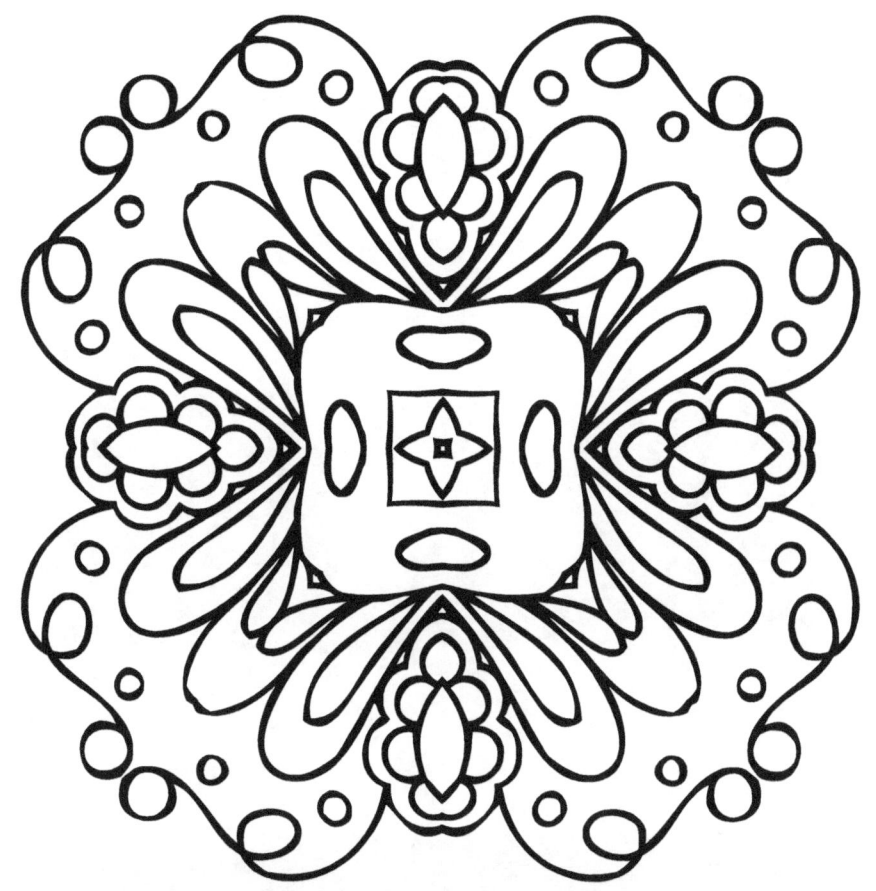

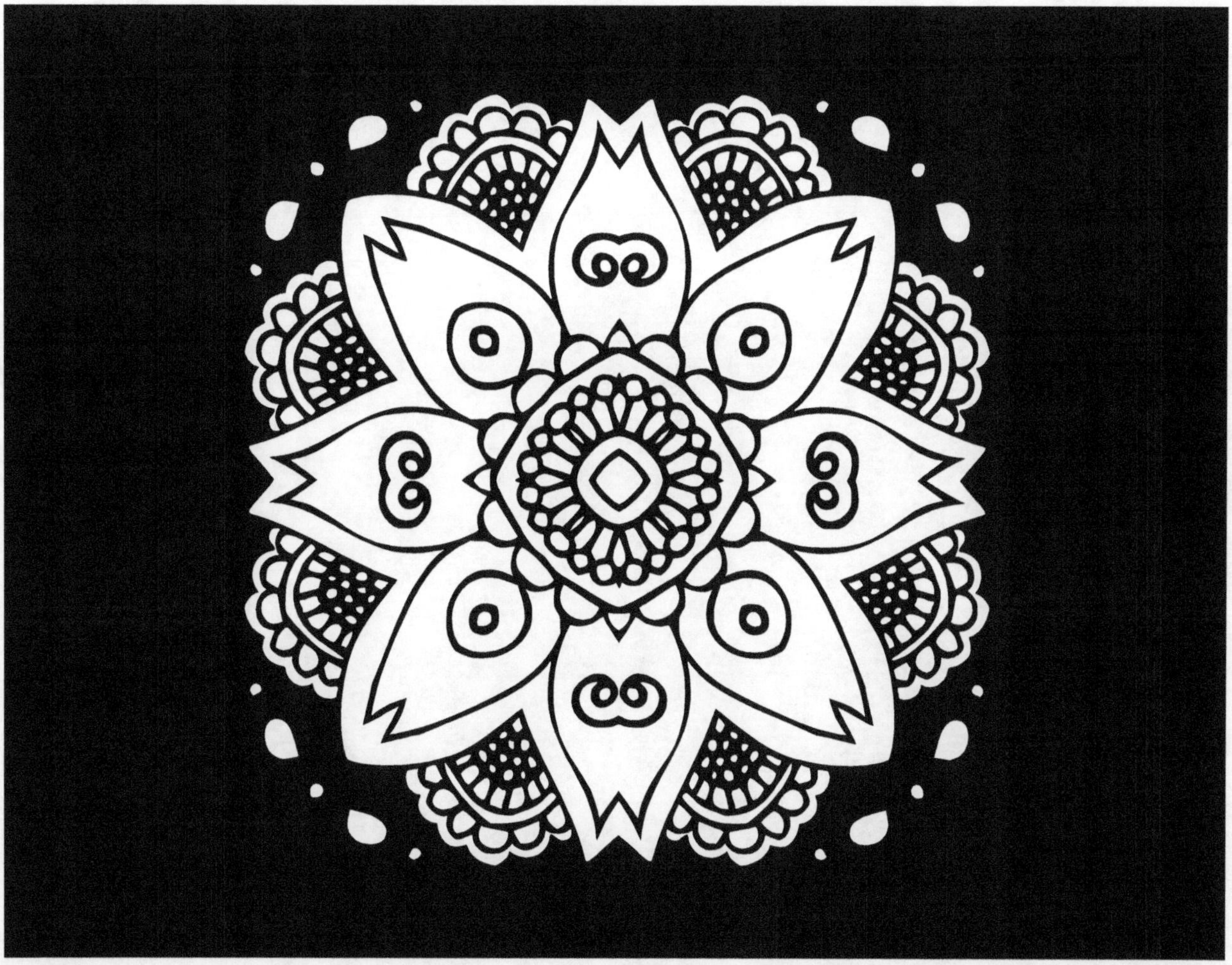

I hope you enjoyed Arthur Rackham's Fairies and Nymphs!

Please take a moment to leave a review on the book's Amazon page.

To find other volumes of Vintage Grayscale Adult Coloring Books, for grayscale coloring tips, to share your colored pages on Facebook, and to find my other adult coloring books, please visit:

ColoringPress.com